A highly informative, instructive and enjoyable account of the life of a great king. Ancient history comes alive in these pages; and there are lessons in compassion and tolerance for today's world.

M.G. Vassanji, *author of* The In-Between World of Vikram Lall

We live today in a spiritual wasteland in which religion is often just the handmaiden of politics. We need to learn from true leaders of history, such as Emperor Ashoka, about the meaning of existence, the way forward as individuals and the way to integrate religion with the social, political and economic systems engulfing us. Ashok Khanna's *Ashoka, the Visionary: Life, Legend and Legacy* is an important beginning step for us to understand the past as a way to make a better future.

Jack Weatherford, *former DeWitt Wallace Professor of anthropology at Macalester College in Minnesota and author of* Genghis Khan and the Making of the Modern World

Ashoka, the Visionary

Ashoka, the Visionary
Life, Legend and Legacy

Ashok Khanna

B L O O M S B U R Y

NEW DELHI • LONDON • OXFORD • NEW YORK • SYDNEY

BLOOMSBURY INDIA
Bloomsbury Publishing India Pvt. Ltd
Second Floor, LSC Building No. 4, DDA Complex, Pocket C – 6 & 7,
Vasant Kunj, New Delhi 110070

BLOOMSBURY, BLOOMSBURY INDIA and the Diana logo are
trademarks of Bloomsbury Publishing Plc

First published in India 2020
This edition published in 2020

ISBN: TPB: 978-93-87457-84-3; eBook: 978-93-87471-21-4

2 4 6 8 10 9 7 5 3 1

Typeset by Manipal Digital System
Printed and bound in India by Replika Press Pvt. Ltd.

To find out more about our authors and books visit www.bloomsbury.com
and sign up for our newsletters

*This book is dedicated to the many friends
who listened to me talking about Ashoka for decades,
and who encouraged me to write his story.*

The fruitfulness of all human activities—many of which are quite worthwhile—relies ultimately on effective governance.

M. McClish and P. Olivelle, paraphrasing Kautilya
in the *Arthasastra*

Contents

Prologue

A Quest and a Cause

With so many books already written about Ashoka, the third ruler of the Mauryan Empire, why am I writing another? There are two reasons: a personal quest and a sense that earlier works have not treated fully or fairly the development of Ashoka's character.

The quest started when I was eight years old, on 15 August 1947, India's Independence Day. My family had an invitation to the flag-changing ceremony, where Lord Louis Mountbatten, the last British viceroy of India and the uncle of Prince Philip, the current Duke of Edinburgh, lowered the Union Jack and Jawaharlal Nehru, India's first prime minister, raised the Indian flag in its place.

Our seats were near the steps that ascended to the platform with the flagpole, at the epicentre of a crowd of one or two million assembled at the edge of Old Delhi, with Jama Masjid visible in the distance. As I had never been in such a huge crowd before, I remember feeling uneasy, but my mother and sister were excited, and their energy infected me as well, though I did not grasp the full significance of the day.

After the ceremony, as the dignitaries mounted the viceroy's horse-drawn carriage, the crowd around us became unruly, pressing against the temporary barriers. I remember the anxiety of that moment. Concerned for our safety, my mother somehow persuaded someone to get us (my mother, sister and myself) onto the livery seat of the vice regal carriage. As we rolled through the tumultuous crowds, waving, Mountbatten lifted me to sit between him and his wife. That thrilling ride, as depicted in these photos, remains deeply imprinted on my soul.

Ashok Khanna with Lord Mountbatten
(*Photo courtesy: Ashok Khanna*)

When we reached the viceroy's palace, Prime Minister Nehru arranged for a car to take us where we needed to go. While waiting for it to arrive, he chatted with us, asked my name, then patted me on the head and said something like, 'Now that India is independent, it's up to young people like you to build it up.' A throwaway line, but one that had a lasting effect on me. Later, I learnt that Nehru had himself been deeply influenced by Emperor Ashoka. Through Nehru, Ashoka's vision of compassionate governance flowed into the Indian Constitution and even onto its flag, where the Ashoka Chakra, a 24-spoke wheel in navy blue, sits at the centre. India's National Emblem, adopted a few months after my meeting with Nehru, is an adaptation of the Ashokan lion capital at Sarnath, also featuring the wheel.

Ashok Khanna with Prime Minister Nehru and Viceroy Lord
Mountbatten (*Photo courtesy: Ashok Khanna*)

As I grew older, I held onto the idea of dedicating my work to India's development. But my first career choice did not fit my temperament. My father was an executive with a prominent British-Indian company; as I had no special career inclination, he steered me toward a university degree in the UK, followed by a professional certification as a chartered accountant. It was a safe, lucrative and prestigious path, but I soon found that I actively disliked the day-to-day work of accounting.

After much turmoil and soul-searching, and attempts at different types of employment in the profession in the UK, Canada and the US, I went back to university in my early thirties. This time, I was determined to find my way back to India. In 1976, armed with graduate business and economics qualifications from Stanford University in addition to undergraduate and professional degrees from the UK, I decided I was ready to make my return. By then, I had pretty much completed the coursework for a doctorate and thought to look for an interesting policy question as a topic for my dissertation.

One day, before I left California, on my usual run at dusk through the hills behind Stanford, a visceral flash revealed in stark clarity my core values: non-violence, reverence for life and acceptance of all ways of life that adhere to those principles. Perhaps it was a powerful 'runner's high', or an insight provoked by the stress of my imminent departure. It might have been considered a spiritual awakening decades ago, though I am more comfortable with the modern psychological term 'peak experience'. Whatever it was, it was certainly powerful. It lingered for decades and shaped how I viewed the world and my place in it, how I chose to earn a living, and how I behaved with people—even how I heard music and saw colours.

Epiphanies come unbidden (and often on hills, if legends are to be trusted). What they spawn may take time to evolve.

In preparation for the move to India, I had been reading Indian history. After my revelation, I wondered if Emperor Ashoka— the greatest ruler of India—had had a similar experience. I felt I finally understood what he meant by a phrase he used in one of his many edicts, which were inscribed on pillars and rocks throughout his domain: 'gift of eye', a kind of insight, a way of looking at the world. And I was struck by how, over a long reign, he sustained a commitment in his edicts to non-violence and tolerance for all religions and living beings, not as a sequestered monk or sadhu (holy man), but in the thick of administering justice and making decisions for an empire all day, every day.

I spent about six months in India, my longest visit since I had left in 1957 to attend college in England. After finding my feet, I interviewed for jobs at public enterprises and academic institutions. I was following the path of Prakash Tandon, an eminent manager and scholar whom I had met a few times, and who had served as a mentor at a distance. I met Prakash in California when he was a visiting professor at Berkeley, and then again on visits to India, while he was the chairman of India's State Trading Corporation and later of Punjab National Bank (he had earlier been the chairman of Hindustan Lever, a prominent multinational company focused on consumer goods). He contributed to the development of professional management in India, both in the private and public sectors, and became a writer. His path in life made sense to me—engage with the world to do something meaningful and then reflect on it in writing. I wanted to follow that trail, as well as I could.

Unfortunately, I was not successful in finding a place for myself. I was rebuffed as a foreigner returning to take scarce jobs away from locals, regardless of my international qualifications. One academic actually yelled at me in anger when I said I was looking for work in his institute. Discouraged, I came back to the US and was lucky to find a position at New York University's Graduate School of Business as a professor. This job came as a boon, because my father had died unexpectedly just before I left India. As the probate process for his will was expected to take about two years, I had to support my mother, who was not savvy about legal or financial matters. The breaks between semesters allowed me to travel to India to assist her. On one of those trips, I honed in on a research topic about India's trade policy for my doctoral dissertation.

As it turned out, my dissertation dovetailed with a substantial research project at the World Bank. That project provided me with additional data and resources that helped me complete my doctorate at last. Soon afterward, I moved to the World Bank in Washington, D.C., to work on industry, trade and finance policies in developing countries. Having failed to contribute to India's development, I was glad to have the chance to do so for other nations. I was also still very much in the thrall of my epiphany, trying to find a way to express those values in my work.

Not naïve about how bureaucracies work, I did my best to concentrate on the substance of my assignments and ignore the manoeuvring within the Bank and client country governments. I agreed with the general thrust of the Bank's policies, based as they were on extensive research, though they did have a measure of ideological bias and a tendency to apply the same solution to all client countries. Nevertheless, I found I had enough wiggle room to tailor aspects of these recommendations to each country's circumstances. It's not easy to customise policy to suit a country's capability and cultural diversity; more attention to this would have raised our effectiveness.

My first significant assignment was to manage policy analyses, and loans based on them, to Kenya. I met and worked with Kenyan officials and politicians for about three years. Although it came as no surprise that several were diverting government funds into their private coffers, it was still jarring. One official frankly said that if others had the opportunity, they would take advantage of it too. The luxurious lifestyle of these officials, with their Mercedes cars and their huge houses in tony suburbs and their private tea gardens, a far cry from the extreme poverty of the vast majority of the population for whose well-being they were responsible, was deeply troubling. The difference between their approach to governance and my understanding of Ashoka was like night and day. Still, despite the dissonance, and like many of my colleagues, I felt that our work contributed to developing the country, making the lives of poor people better, faster. I accepted that rationalisation to make my position palatable.

Unexpectedly, a few years later, I got to work on reforming India's financial system for about three years. Thrilled, I took this as an opportunity to fulfil the responsibility that Prime Minister Nehru had assigned me with on Independence Day. As I knew a few people who had returned to India as senior advisors to the government, I felt hopeful that I would not encounter the poor governance that I'd seen in Kenya.

But India turned out to be my worst assignment while on staff at the World Bank. Being of Indian origin, I was expected to understand colloquial language and gestures that I was no longer familiar with; perhaps my lack of understanding gave the false impression of a haughty, foreign-educated attitude. Indian officials, meanwhile, did everything possible not to have their policy errors and corruption exposed and addressed. The result of our team's analytical work was sensitive, as it brought to light an enormous failure of earlier Indian policies. The level of governance in the government-owned banks was abysmal. They were corrupt, inefficient and insolvent, and needed to be bailed out at the taxpayer's expense. Instead of contributing to India's development, they were a millstone, slowing it down. The World Bank's suggested reforms would have highlighted these failures; to avoid facing up to them, Indian officials attempted to compromise me personally. They threatened to lobby against me at the Bank, tried to bribe me with a prestigious job in India, and even made efforts to entrap me into making statements that would adversely affect my standing with my bosses.

Deeply disappointed, I resigned from the World Bank when it became clear that our work had hit the wall of the government's unwillingness to recognise the problem and proceed with much-needed reforms. Minuscule reforms have since been implemented, but it has come to light recently that India's public banking system is just as rotten as it was in 1990, except with larger losses. A recent speech the current chief of India's Prime Minister's Economic Advisory Council gave at a seminar at Stanford University revealed that the lame excuses given for the slow pace of reform are the same as those used decades ago. If I could, I would like to tell Prime Minister Nehru that I tried to contribute to India's development, and to apologise for having been so ineffective.

Working on development remained the best way to express my values, and the flexible travel allowed me to meet family responsibilities that spread from D.C. to New Delhi. Although I was no longer on staff at the World Bank, I continued as a consultant to do the same kind of policy analysis for it and one of its sister organisations, the Asian Development Bank, in a variety of countries in Asia, Eastern Europe, Africa and South America. Poor governance was pervasive, with the result that efforts to alleviate poverty or provide basic services were stymied.

Ashoka's visionary inscriptions came to mind time and again. More than two millennia ago, he had attempted to provide compassionate and effective governance. His efforts inspired many rulers in Buddhist Asia to emulate him. Reviving his story, I often thought, could provide an example for contemporary governments to follow.

I began to research Ashoka's life and works and, whenever possible, I visited sites related to him or the rulers he inspired. Sarnath and Sanchi, in India, and Lumbini, in Nepal, were particularly moving. Although these sites are dedicated to Buddha, Ashoka's presence can be felt in the pillars and inscriptions, perhaps most of all in the magnificent lion capital at Sarnath. The monuments in Polonnaruwa, in Sri Lanka, Shewdagon Paya, in Myanmar, That Luang, in Laos, Bayon, in Cambodia, Ayutthaya, in Thailand, and Borobudur, in Indonesia, made a deep impression on me, as well.

As my research continued, the second motivation for this book began to develop. When I reflected on the many books I'd read, I concluded that Ashoka as a person, rather than as a ruler, had not been understood well. Other than his inscriptions, there is virtually no remaining evidence of his personal life. Historians have used legends written centuries after his death to present him as a two-dimensional stock figure: a cruel emperor with a torture chamber, who put to death ministers who disobeyed him and concubines who avoided him. But after his first and only war, eight years into his reign, he is thought to have converted to Buddhism, and become enlightened.

There are two main legends that tell his story, both written by Buddhists centuries after his reign. The *Asokavadana*, the legend of Ashoka, written in Sanskrit in the second century CE, is the main text of the Northern Buddhist Tradition prevalent in North West India and, in translation, in Central Asia, China,

Korea, Japan and Tibet. The *Mahavamsa*, the great chronicle, written in Pali in the fifth century CE, is the main text of the Southern Buddhist Tradition, prevalent in Sri Lanka, Myanmar, Thailand and other parts of South East Asia. Through much of history since Ashoka's time, he has been known only through these collected legends, which may contain elements of historical truth mixed with a great deal of fictionalised detail, as legends about renowned historical figures usually do. The purpose of the collections was not to provide historical accounts, but to celebrate Ashoka as a great and mighty Buddhist king, who had experienced a remarkable religious conversion and thereafter exemplified the ideals of the communities that created the two epics. (They also display a suspicion of secular rulers in their pre-conversion narratives). They seem most reliable when they conform to Ashoka's edicts' promotion of a civil *Dhamma*—a set of ethical principles of social behaviour and governance based on Buddhist philosophical foundations.

From age forty-two to about fifty-seven, he composed nearly thirty inscriptions addressing non-violence, tolerance of all religions and governing with compassion. Based on one legend, some historians suggest he continued to be a cruel ruler during this period, killing thousands who followed his mother's and grandfather's religions. They paint him as a person with a split personality—preaching tolerance and non-violence while killing people who subscribed to religions other than Buddhism. These interpretations, though, are too simplistic. Instead, we should interpret the legends by asking how they fit with the clear views indicated in Ashoka's edicts, the only real evidence of his life and rule.

Any portrait of Ashoka requires a degree of imagination. Much of his life has been lost to time. But I believe that reading the edicts and the legends together, alongside recent contemporary research, can give us the fullest picture possible of who he was. Thus, in this book, I will attempt to draw a balanced picture of a ruler who sought to create a compassionate civilisation in which all citizens were treated equally and could thrive, and whose influence has been pervasive in Asia ever since.

Chronology*

599–527	Mahavira, founder of Jainism
563–483	Gautama Buddha
350–275	Chanakya (advisor and chief minister to Chandragupta)
326–324	Alexander's invasion of Hindush
326/325	Chandragupta, the founder of the Mauryan Empire, possibly meets Alexander
321–297	Chandragupta's reign, with the capital in Pataliputra, Magadha, in modern Bihar (East India), and Chanakya as his chief minister
305/303	Chandragupta's battle against Seleucus I Nicator (successor to Alexander in Asia), concluded with a peace treaty
303–300	Megasthenes, ambassador of Seleucus, visits Chandragupta's court in Pataliputra
300	Ashoka's birth
297	Chandragupta abdicates. Bindusara, his son, becomes emperor
297–272	Bindusara's reign
282	Ashoka sent to Taxila to help his elder brother Sushima quell a rebellion

* The years are in BCE and are approximate; historians do not agree precisely.

282–272   Ashoka is viceroy at Ujjain, the capital of the empire's central province. He meets and cohabits with Devi; they have two children, Mahinda and Sanghamitta.

272–269/8   Interregnum after Bindusara's death and Ashoka's accession with the help of Radhagupta, who then becomes his chief minister

269/8–232   Ashoka's reign

260   War against Kalinga (modern state of Odisha)

259/8   Ashoka's first Dhamma yatra (tour of piety) for 256 days to the Bodhi Tree in Bodh Gaya (about 50 miles south of Pataliputra), where the Buddha achieved enlightenment; issues Rock Edicts III, IV, & VIII; issues Minor Rock Edict I (Lay Buddhist); Gift of Caves at Nyagrodha and Khalatika to Ajivika

257   Fourteen Rock Edicts; Bhabra (Second Bairat) Rock Edict

256   Rock Edict XIII (Kalinga War)

255   Rock Edicts completed; Separate Rock Edict; Schism Edict; appointment of Dhamma *Mahamattas* (Ashoka's ministers for preaching Dhamma and administering charity)

250   Third Buddhist Council ends in Pataliputra; missions sent all over the empire and to foreign lands

248   Ashoka visits Lumbini, Buddha's birthplace; visits stupa at Kanakamuni; issues Pillar Edicts at Rummindei and Niglivia

243   Issues Pillar Edicts I-VII

241   Asandhimitta, Ashoka's chief queen, dies

236   Tissarakha made chief queen

232   Ashoka's death

CHAPTER 1

Ashoka's Epiphany

The Dhauli Hills rise from the banks of the Daya River, about six miles south of Bhubaneswar, capital of the modern state of Odisha in East India. The hills overlook an expanse of lush green rice paddies stretching toward the horizon, with the river winding through them.

In ancient times, this land was in the Kingdom of Kalinga. Ashoka may have stood atop one of these hills to command the mighty Mauryan army in a battle against Kalinga that took place around 260 BCE. Although Kalinga's army was formidable, it was no match for the powerful, battle-tested Mauryan juggernaut, undefeated for half a century, even in battle against Seleucus Nicator, Alexander's successor in Asia.

Ashoka hoped, indeed expected, that Kalinga's king and generals, seeing the overwhelming strength of the Mauryan forces, would sue for peace and accept Mauryan suzerainty, as many kingdoms in the subcontinent had done. When no sign of surrender appeared, however, he reluctantly gave the order to advance.

The engagement began with both adversaries softening their enemy with showers of arrows shot from longbows. With overwhelming superiority in numbers and arms, the Mauryans adopted an 'eagle formation', their seasoned troops at the beak, accompanied by war elephants with swordlike weapons attached to their trunks. As they charged into Kalinga's lines, cavalry at the tips of the wings galloped to surround the opposing formation. Chariots with scythes attached to their wheels, carrying archers and javelin throwers, advanced from the wings as well, closely followed by the infantry.

After initial stiff resistance, Kalinga's lines broke. Its forces fled in disorder. The Mauryan army closed the pincer and surrounded them, slaughtering their foes with broadswords and javelins. The churned fields were covered with body parts, discarded weapons and blood. As the slaughter spread into the river, it turned from muddy brown to dirty red. Tens of thousands of dead Kalingan soldiers lay scattered across the fields and floating in the water. Many more were wounded, some shouting for help, others resigned to their fate or quietly limping and crawling to safety. Later, families arrived to scour the area in search of husbands, brothers and children, wailing in sorrow when they found them or leaving silently in relief when they did not.

Ashoka watched the field for hours after the battle ended, horrified by the devastation. He had tried to stop the slaughter, but it had all happened too quickly. He gave an order to cease fighting and take prisoners, but it couldn't reach most field commanders, and if it did, they failed to transmit it to the ranks. The battlefield was in the grip of chaos. The massacre had its own inexorable momentum.

Ashoka ignored the congratulations of his generals and the ensuing victory celebration. He refused to leave his command podium. He alone had caused the barbaric killing. It was his responsibility. Deeply remorseful, he swore he would not see such a scene again. He mourned for the dead and lamented the suffering inflicted on their families and friends.

The war against Kalinga was a turning point for Ashoka, the moment of his identity crisis, in psychologist Erik Erikson's sense. With that epiphany on the hill, Ashoka began his journey toward becoming an enlightened ruler who preached non-violence, tolerance of all religions and good governance for the rest of his long reign. Over the next few years, he became an ardent Buddhist, adopting the religion as his philosophical foundation and the ethical basis for governing his empire. He developed a code of social ethics (a social religion, in effect) and called it Dhamma.

There is no historical record of Ashoka commanding or watching the battle, but the earlier account is how I imagine it based on his thirteenth rock edict, quoted later. No other victorious monarch in human history has expressed so clearly his remorse for those killed and injured in battle:

> *Beloved-of-the-Gods, King Piyadasi* [a title used for Ashoka in his edicts], *conquered the Kalingas eight years after his coronation. One hundred and fifty thousand were deported, one hundred thousand were killed, and many more (died from other causes). After the Kalingas had been conquered, Beloved-of-the-Gods came to feel a strong inclination toward the Dhamma, a love for the Dhamma and for instruction in Dhamma. Now Beloved-of-the-Gods feels deep remorse for having conquered the Kalingas.*
>
> *Indeed, Beloved-of-the-Gods is deeply pained by the killing, dying, and deportation that take place when an unconquered country is conquered. But Beloved-of-the-Gods is pained even more by this—that Brahmans, ascetics, and householders of different religions who live in those countries, and who are respectful to superiors, to mother and father, to elders, and who behave properly and have strong loyalty toward friends,*

*acquaintances, companions, relatives, servants and employees—
that they are injured, killed or separated from their loved ones.
Even those who are not affected (by all this) suffer when they see
friends, acquaintances, companions and relatives affected. These
misfortunes befall all (as a result of war) and this pains Beloved-
of-the-Gods.*

*There is no country, except among the Greeks, where these
two groups, Brahmans and ascetics, are not found, and there is no
country where people are not devoted to one or another religion.
Therefore, the killing, death or deportation of a hundredth, or
even a thousandth, part of those who died during the conquest of
Kalinga now pains Beloved-of-the-Gods. Now Beloved-of-the-
Gods thinks that even those who do wrong should be forgiven
where forgiveness is possible.*

*Even the forest people, who live in Beloved-of-the-Gods'
domain, are entreated and reasoned with to act properly. They
are told that despite his remorse Beloved-of-the-Gods has the
power to punish them if necessary, so that they should be ashamed
of their wrong and not be killed. Truly, Beloved-of-the-Gods
desires non-injury, restraint, and impartiality to all beings, even
where wrong has been done.*

*Now it is conquest by Dhamma that Beloved-of-the-Gods
considers to be the best conquest. And it (conquest by Dhamma)
has been won here, on the borders, even six hundred yojanas (a
measure of distance equivalent to about eight miles) away, where
the Greek king Antiochos rules, and beyond there where the four
kings named Ptolemy, Antigonos, Magas and Alexander rule,
and likewise in the south among the Cholas, the Pandyas and as
far as Tamraparni. Here in the king's domain among the Greeks,
the Kambojas, the Nabhakas, the Nabhapamkits, the Bhojas, the
Pitinikas, the Andhras, and the Palidas, everywhere people are
following Beloved-of-the-Gods' instructions in Dhamma. Even
where Beloved-of-the-Gods' envoys have not been, these people
too, having heard of the practice of Dhamma and the ordinances
and instructions in Dhamma given by Beloved-of-the-Gods,
are following it and will continue to do so. This conquest has*

been won everywhere, and it gives great joy—the joy which only conquest by Dhamma can give. But even this joy is of little consequence. Beloved-of-the-Gods considers the great fruit to be experienced in the next world to be more important.

I have had this Dhamma edict written so that my sons and great-grandsons may not consider making new conquests, or that if military conquests are made, that they be done with forbearance and light punishment, or better still, that they consider making conquest by Dhamma only, for that bears fruit in this world and the next. May all their intense devotion be given to this, which has a result in this world and the next.1

The site of the historical battle between Kalinga and the Mauryan Empire, and the place of Ashoka's epiphany, is a destination for Buddhist pilgrimage because of his edicts. At the top of the hill is the imposing white Shanti (Peace) Stupa, built in the 1970s by two Japanese sanghas.

CHAPTER 2
Ashoka, an Introduction

Ashoka Maurya was the third ruler of the dynasty established by his grandfather Chandragupta Maurya in 322 BCE. Ashoka was born in about 300 BCE and ruled as emperor from about 269 to 232 BCE. He governed a vast region stretching over a million square miles (today's India, except for the southern cone, plus Pakistan and Afghanistan), which was populated by nomadic, diverse peoples who practiced many religions. For several decades after his conquest of Kalinga, the region was peaceful and prosperous.

Many historians and writers have rated Ashoka as the greatest monarch of India and among the greatest rulers in human history. Rabindranath Tagore, the world-renowned, Nobel Prize-winning poet and musician, observed that 'countless great kingdoms of countless great monarchs have suffered devastation and been razed to dust, but the glorious emergence of the power of benevolence in Asoka has become our proud asset, and is breathing strength into us.' H.G. Wells commented in *The Outline of History*: 'Amidst the tens of thousands of names of monarchs that crowd the columns of history, their majesties, and graciousnesses and serenities and royal highnesses and the like, the name of Ashoka shines, and shines almost alone, a star. From the Volga to Japan, his name is still honoured. China, Tibet, and even India, though it has left his doctrine, preserve the tradition of his greatness.'[1] Jawaharlal Nehru, in his *The Discovery of India*, describes Ashoka as 'a man who was greater than any king or emperor'.

The distinguished Indian historian Beni Madhab Barua declared that 'Asoka did for the religion of the Buddha what Darius the Great or Xerxes had done for that of the Avesta and St. Paul did for that of Christ. He indeed raised Buddhism from the position of a local faith to the status of a world religion.'[2] The internationally renowned world religions scholar Huston Smith, in a book written with Philip Novak, said: 'In the history of ancient royalty [Ashoka's] figure stands out like a Himalayan peak, clear and resplendent against a sunlit sky. If we are not all Buddhists today, it was not Ashoka's fault. Not content to become a follower of the Buddha himself, he commended the Dharma energetically yet non-violently across a vast Indian empire stretching to three continents…. His widely disseminated edicts… dismissed empty ritual and warned against cruelty, anger, and pride while extolling in their place generosity, tolerance, truthfulness, kindness to human and non-human animals, and vigour in pursuing the awakened life…. Finding Buddhism an Indian sect, he left it a world religion.'[3]

Buddha found the path to end human suffering and achieved enlightenment deep in meditation, removed from the world. Ashoka followed Buddha's path deep in the world, revealing a shining example of non-violent, tolerant, efficient and considerate governance. He ruled for about thirty-five years, in which time he transformed Buddhism from a small local sect into a world religion. Buddhism grew even after Ashoka promulgated his own secular code of social ethics (Dhamma), probably developed to convey even-handed treatment for all religions. The contemporary scholar John Strong says that 'the Asokan [sic] state was to be governed according to Dharma [sic]. The people were to follow Dharma. Wars of aggression were to be replaced by conquests of Dharma. Special royal ministers were charged with the propagation of Dharma... the old royal pleasure-tours and hunts were replaced by Dharma-pilgrimages.... Dharma seems to have meant for Asoka [sic] a moral polity of active social concern, religious tolerance, ecological awareness, the observance of common ethical precepts, and the renunciation of war.'[4] In historian Nayanjot Lahiri's review of early biographies of Ashoka by Smith and Bhandarkar in her recent book, she reports their belief that Ashoka was second only to Buddha in the history of Buddhism.[5]

Ashoka had an extraordinary reverence for all living beings. He used this understanding to rule his empire, fusing ethics with the exercise of power, preaching non-violence and tolerance, and exhorting against animal sacrifice. He himself became a vegetarian. While he emphasised economic growth and improved communications, he was also mindful of environmental concerns some 2,000 years before they became commonplace.

He was a great administrator—promoting justice, checking the abuse of power, protecting the disadvantaged, implementing prison reform and encouraging the growth of medicinal herbs. He had an international outlook, incorporating Persian and Greek ideas (and people) into his administration. Art attained a high standard. Notable buildings were richly adorned with decorative patterns and a wide variety of bas-reliefs, along with numerous statues of people and animals.

His influence on governance has been long and abiding, setting an example that was followed by rulers throughout Asia, from India to Japan. More recently, according to Lahiri, Indian national leaders who joined Gandhi in the struggle for independence looked up to Ashoka as the ultimate inspiration of their movement. Ashoka influenced modern India's Constitution through Nehru. His impact was felt in Myanmar through U Nu, and in Cambodia through Prince Norodom Sihanouk.

Despite these appraisals and accomplishments, Ashoka is not as famous as Alexander the Great, Caesar, Genghis Khan or Napoleon. Even in India, Rama, a mythical king, enjoys wide recognition and adulation, but Ashoka, a real historical person, is barely known beyond academia.[6] One reason for this lack of recognition is that his biographies have been written by academic historians, in language and detail that is difficult for non-academic readers to digest. One of my objectives for this book is to remedy that lacuna.

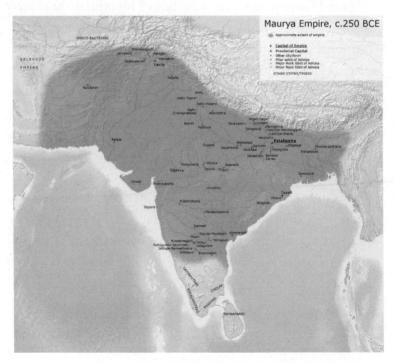

Mauryan Empire
(Photo courtesy: Wikimedia Commons)

Here are some of Ashoka's words, taken from edicts carved on pillars and rocks:

Non-violence

'His majesty feels remorse, sorrow, and regret on account of the conquest because of the slaughter, death and people taken captive.... The loss of a hundredth or thousandth part of those slaughtered, carried away would now be a matter of deep regret.'

Tolerance: 'Man must not do reverence to his own sect by disparaging that of another's for trivial reasons. Other people's sects deserve reverence. By acting in this way, a man exalts his own sect and at the same time does service to the sects of other people.'

Good Governance: Ashoka exhorted his officials 'to observe the moral rule. Individuals have been put in prison undeservedly. You must be at hand to stop unwarranted imprisonment and torture.' He appointed ombudsmen to 'engage in promoting the welfare and happiness of all.... They are engaged in the prevention of wrongful imprisonment or chastisement, in the work of removing hindrances and deliverance, considering cases where a man has a large family, has been smitten by calamity.'

In Rock Edict VI, Ashoka sums up his governing dedication: 'I consider the welfare of all to be my duty.... There is no better work than promoting the welfare of all the people and whatever effort I am making is to repay the debt I owe to all beings to assure their happiness in this life, and attain heaven in the next.'[7]

CHAPTER 3

Discovering Ashoka

Reconstructing Ashoka's life story and vision is a fascinating and complex adventure.

There are no surviving texts about Ashoka from his lifetime, other than his own edicts, which are the most significant sources we have for our understanding of his views, as well as of his travels within his kingdom. But this lacuna is far from unusual for prominent ancient figures. There are no contemporaneous accounts of the Buddha, Krishna, Mahavira, Zoroaster, Moses, King David, Socrates, Jesus, etc.—there are only the accounts of disciples, followers, communities and historians after, and most often long after, their deaths.

The Buddha's story and teachings are transmitted accounts of his followers. Scholars regard Krishna as an actual historical figure, but he is known to us only through later religious literature such as the Mahabharata, which depicts him as the incarnation of Vishnu. Mahavira, who established Jainism as the religion we know today, with its commitment to non-violence, is believed to have been born in the sixth century BCE to a royal family in the North of modern-day Patna, the eventual capital of the Mauryan Empire. He is thought to have renounced his wealth and status to commit himself to asceticism and then to the preaching of what he regarded as core ethical principles. He is believed by both Jains and Buddhists to have been a contemporary of the Buddha, and their stories have striking parallels, including the one on attaining enlightenment under a tree. But his actual life history and teachings are known only through later religious texts and legends. Zoroaster, another influential religious teacher, is even more shrouded in obscurity. He is known to us through religious texts he is alleged to have written and subsequent legendary accounts, but scholars have estimated his time period to have been anywhere from 1500 to 500 BCE.

Some historians even doubt the existence of Moses, and regard the biblical account of the escape of the Israelites from Egypt and their forty-year trek through the Arabian Desert to the Promised Land of Palestine to be a compelling mythological account of a much longer, complex process by which the Israelites invaded and conquered the native population and eventually incorporated the native people's gods into the multifaceted features of their supreme Yahweh. King David's story is known only from much later biblical accounts that, like all such accounts, reflect the interests of the surviving community writing them.

Socrates's teachings and story come to us through his student Plato's accounts and through the references of later Greek playwrights. Jesus is known because of the preaching and accounts of figures like Paul, who didn't know the historical Jesus but preached the salvific power of Christ. The first of the New Testament books, Mark, was written around the year 70 CE, and evidently incorporated sayings that circulated earlier. There are minor references to Jesus and his followers by Josephus and other Roman writers, which verify his historicity but not his followers' accounts.

And Ashoka? The only 'concrete' evidence we have are the edicts inscribed on pillars and rocks during his time, but they provide much more contemporary confirmations of his convictions than the surviving accounts of comparable legendary historical figures. As with Moses, David and Jesus, there are also much later stories about Ashoka that blend historical reality with mythologising and ideological intents.

The two Buddhist literary texts mentioned earlier, the *Asokavadana* and the *Mahavamsa*, written centuries after his reign, supplement the edicts.[1] The veracity and biases of these works, and their similarities and differences, continue to be debated by scholars.

The *Mahavamsa* was discovered in the early nineteenth century by British administrators in Sri Lanka, who believed in aligning their administration with the mores of their colony's native citizens. The enlightened lawyer Alexander Johnston, as advocate general and then as chief justice, abolished the slave trade on the island, instituted trial by jury and advocated universal education. He also studied the laws of the island's religions and communities, in the course of which he came across the *Mahavamsa* written in the original Pali.

Around this same time, the Methodist missionary William Buckley Fox arrived in Sri Lanka and quickly became, as per Alexander Johnston, the best Pali and Sinhalese scholar of the time. Johnston asked Fox to translate the *Mahavamsa*, which Fox proceeded to do, though he likely worked from a Sinhalese translation of a flawed Pali text. It was Fox's translation that revealed to the West the existence of the Sri Lankan King Petissa II, who was convinced by the Indian monarch Darmasoca to embrace Buddhism, thereby establishing Sri Lanka as a Buddhist country ever since.

Although the edicts were still known early in the Common Era, it now seems clear that within a few centuries of Ashoka's death, people no longer knew the script in which they were written and, thus, were unable to understand what they said. By the fourteenth century CE, even the connection to Ashoka had been forgotten. Over the centuries, various reports and historical records—from Chinese Buddhist pilgrims, Persian conquerors, Mongolian and Mughal invaders, and then from British officials who were also remarkable scholars—marvelled at the inscribed pillars and rocks, but did not understand them.

As will be discussed more fully later, the Chinese Buddhist monks Faxian (in the fourth century) and Xuanzang (in the seventh century) undertook long journeys of discovery to what had once been Ashoka's vast realm. Both monks wrote travelogues that include descriptions of inscribed Ashokan pillars. Locals allegedly told the monks what they believed the engravings said, but it seems clear that the informants could not really read them, and instead gave the monks interpretations that would please the pilgrims' Buddhist sensibilities.

In the fourteenth century, the Turkic Sultan Firoz Shah Tughlaq encountered some beautifully polished and inscribed Ashokan pillars in modern Ambala district. He had them hauled to Delhi, which he was having rebuilt, and ordered that they be prominently erected. Firoz Shah was born of an Indian mother, who raised him alone after his father died prematurely. That upbringing may well have been a crucial factor in his unusual religious tolerance and relatively peaceful character. His restoration of what his fellow Muslims regarded as pagan ruins seemed almost heretical to many at his court; earlier Muslim conquerors had been aware of Ashokan pillars, but had destroyed rather than preserved them. Firoz Shah not only preserved them, but went to great lengths to try to understand them, consulting with Brahmans and other Hindus to learn what the inscriptions said. Still, no one could decipher them.

After Firoz Shah's time, the Mongol invasions began. The first Turkish Mongolian ruler in India was Timur, a Muslim descendant of Genghis Khan, who later became well known in the West as Tamburlaine, an outsize figure in retellings ranging from Christopher Marlowe's sixteenth-century *Tamburlaine the Great* to a twenty-first century BBC radio play. Although his reign in Persia and India was violent and destructive, Timur was surprised and delighted by the tall gold inscribed Ashokan pillar with a lion on top that he discovered in Delhi, amid his razing of the city. He declared it to be the most remarkable monument that he had ever encountered.

A few centuries later, the British continued the rediscovery of Ashoka's inscribed pillars and rocks all over the Mauryan dynasty's ancient realm. In the sixteenth century, the English merchant William Finch came across the gold pillar in Delhi; he and his associates speculated that the inscription must have been in a kind of Greek and attributed it to Alexander, who had invaded India before Ashoka's time. John Marshall, an agent of the British East India Company, set out in the seventeenth century to find more Ashokan pillars.

However, it was not until 1836 that the brilliant English polymath James Prinsep was able to begin to decipher and translate the Brahmi script in which most of the edicts were written, and to publish his translations in the *Journal of the Asiatic Society,* of which he was the editor. And since the edicts do not use Ashoka's name, but one of his titles—King Devanampriya Piyadasi—Prinsep assumed that King Devanampriya Tissa of Sri Lanka had created them. It was George Turnour, a British colonial administrator, scholar and translator in Sri Lanka at the time, who identified King Devanampriya Piyadasi as Ashoka, based on his having translated the *Mahavamsa,* in which Ashoka is given that title. It turned out the legends ended up providing a crucial component of our understanding of the edicts as concrete evidence of Ashoka's reign.

Other evidence comes from the works of Megasthenes, a Macedonian ambassador to the court of Chandragupta (Ashoka's grandfather). His writing is lost, but he was quoted by Greek commentators such as Strabo and Diodorus Siculus (first century BCE) and Arrian (second century CE) and by the Roman writer Pliny (first century CE). Until recently, authors also drew on the *Arthasastra* by Kautilya, thinking it was about the Mauryan Empire. Many historians have now concluded that it was composed between 100 BCE and 100 CE, well after Ashoka's dynasty ended its rule over India. Mark McClish and Patrick Olivelle argue that the text assumes a small, regional empire rather than the vast Mauryan realm and that its discussion of the minting of coins reflects the realities of at least two centuries after Ashoka's reign.[2] Nayanjot Lahiri, though, questions their conclusions and holds that the *Arthasastra*'s core was almost certainly composed around the time of Chandragupta—she does not, though, define what the core is. She contends that the text describes a type of administration that seems appropriate for a large political area, or for the metropolitan areas of an empire. Lahiri also finds remarkable similarities between some of the *Arthasastra*'s counsel and that of Ashoka—for instance, the ruler's responsibility to maintain the well-being of his subjects through the provision of healthcare, support for agriculture, etc., and to be accessible and in communication with his people via local representatives.[3]

It could well be that the *Arthasastra*, like other ancient texts, reflects multiple time periods. The Gospels of Mark and John, for instance, were not written by the actual apostles but by heritage communities who continued their testimony as handed down through decades of stories, oral and written, honouring their founding apostles with their attributions. The *Arthasastra* may well incorporate elements dating back to the Mauryan era, despite having been composed centuries later.

Another text, the woodblock-printed *The History of Buddhism in India* by the Tibetan lama, Taranatha, who lived in Mongolia in the seventeenth century CE, seems to rely on much older sources as well, and includes three chapters on Ashoka. Although the reliability of its history is highly questionable, it may still contain stories that reflect historical reality. Like other texts, it relates Ashoka's Mauryan lineage, celebrates his conversion from an evil life to one of Buddhist munificence and his convening of the great Buddhist Council, and recounts his Buddhist mentor's instructions to collect relics of the Buddha and to construct 84,000 stupas.

French scholars, meanwhile, finally translated the journals of Faxian and Xuanzang in the nineteenth century, adding more to the picture. Decades of debate and discussion among historians sifting through these and other sources have yielded a reasonable consensus about Ashoka's chronology, his works and his devotion to Buddhism. But speculation remains about who he was as a person, and how he evolved into a great ruler.

Among the many modern books written about Ashoka, Romila Thapar's *Asoka and the Decline of the Mauryas* is the most comprehensive and balanced review of the historical evidence. American scholar John Strong's introduction to and translation of the *Asokavadana* in *The Legend of King Asoka* is expertly informative and replete with stories about the emperor. The southern legends are presented to us in *Mahavamsa: The Great Chronicle of Ceylon*, translated by Wilhelm Geiger with Mabel Haynes Bode; they emphasise Ashoka's Buddhist convictions, which led to the sending of two of his children, who were Buddhist monks, to Sri Lanka. Due to their efforts, India's island neighbour remains primarily Buddhist till today. Assessing the credibility of the legends about Ashoka is difficult, but those accounts that conform to the character and policies laid out in the edicts from his own lifetime should be given more weight, as the edicts are the only hard evidence available to us.

Two conference volumes to which the aforementioned authors (along with other scholars) contributed—*King Asoka and Buddhism: Historical and Literary Studies* and, more recently, *Reimagining Asoka*—widened and updated the net of knowledge about the emperor. Charles Allen's *Ashoka: The Search for India's Lost Emperor* provides a detailed account of the discoveries and ultimate decoding of the edicts, but devotes only about forty or so pages to Ashoka's life story and his extensive influence through history. Lahiri's recently published comprehensive history, *Ashoka in Ancient India,* provides valuable information about the archaeological sites associated with him, further enhancing our knowledge and fuelling the ongoing interest in his life and vision.

CHAPTER 4

Ashoka's Origins

To understand Ashoka's reign, it is important to know about the Indian, Persian and Macedonian history that preceded his ascent.

The Mauryan Empire established by Ashoka's grandfather Chandragupta did not arise in isolation from the rest of the then civilised world. Indeed, according to the historian D.P. Singhal, 'during the early part of the Mauryan administration, palace organisation, court etiquette and deportment were still greatly influenced by ideas and models from the Persian Empire— even the Mauryan idea of empire was perhaps inspired by that example. The imperialism of the Mauryan monarchy, especially of Ashoka, was a synthesis of Indian, Achaemenian [Persian] and Hellenistic ideas.'[1]

Aryan Migration

Perhaps the story starts in about 2000 BCE, when a conquering migration of Central Asian Aryan-speaking people moved in waves to Iran and India, to their south and east, and to Greece and Germany, to their west and north. By about 1500 BCE, these migrants had established themselves in their new territories. Aryan speech with local variations, now known as Indo-European, supplanted local languages. These migrants brought their gods with them, as well, and passed them on to their descendants: the Iranian God Mithra and the Vedic Mitra were originally identical, and the Zoroastrian deity Ahura is called Varuna in the Vedas. The Greek gods of heaven, Zeus and Uranus, are the Vedic Dyaus and Varuna. The Vedic religion has much in common with Zoroastrianism and Vedic Sanskrit closely resembles the language of the Zoroastrian Avesta. Although the Persians, Greeks and Indians shared the same linguistic and religious roots, that ancestry was eventually forgotten; they met as strangers under the Persian Empire.

Persian Empire

By 547 BCE, Cyrus, founder of the Persian Empire, had captured Media and Lydia, where he made the first direct contact with Ionian (Eastern) Greeks, who had settled in West Asia a few centuries earlier. By 539 BCE, he had also captured Elam and Babylon, and ruled a region stretching from Gandhara and Bactria (modern Afghanistan) in the east to the Ionian cities in the west. Seventeen years and three rulers later, Darius I expanded the Persian Empire still further, to encompass Egypt in the west and Hindush (Pakistan), with its capital at Taxila, in the east, after he sponsored the Greek explorer Scylax's expedition down the Indus in 510 BCE.

Hindush paid an annual tribute of 360 talents of gold dust to the empire, about one-third of its total revenues. When Alexander visited Taxila, it was the most prosperous city in the fertile region between the Indus and Hydaspes (Jhelum) rivers. According to Singhal, 'No country he [Alexander] had hitherto visited was so populous and well cultivated, or abounded in so many valuable productions of nature and art, as that part of India through which he led his army.'[2]

Darius I introduced sweeping reforms to the Persian administration and legal system. He reorganised the empire into twenty satrapies, elevated Persians to work alongside locals in all branches of administration and installed laws based on Hammurabi's Code. (Hammurabi ruled Babylon from 1792 to1750 BCE and issued laws, carved on a stele, instituting rules of contractual and social relations that tried to establish equality, but still favoured the upper classes.)

Persian Empire
(Image courtesy: Adobe Stock)

Darius also standardised weights, measures and coinage, and extended their use. He introduced a balanced tax system to levy dues on production and distribution, and created a network of well-maintained roads to improve movement within the empire, critical for its management. Ports and quays were constructed for the first time and fixed buoys were available for mooring ships. These improvements facilitated trade, which expanded during his reign, and boosted economic growth.[3] While the architecture and art of Darius's successor Xerxes have been deemed more refined, Darius's contributions were significant. He built palaces in Susa and Persepolis with materials obtained from all parts of the empire.

Darius also used inscriptions to promulgate his authority and laws. He had his autobiography engraved on the Behistun rock, a history of his ascension to the throne, his conquests and rebellions against his rule, accompanied by a life-sized bas-relief of himself. In keeping with the grandiose palace architecture, the king's lifestyle was also monumental. On one of his birthdays, he entertained 15,000 guests.

Greeks and Indians in the Persian Empire

Cyrus's conquest of the Greek Ionian cities led to substantial contact between the Greeks and other subjects of the Persian Empire. Greek philosophers and physicians, such as Ctesias, who lived at the Persian court for seventeen years, travelled throughout the empire; several prominent European Greek leaders from Athens and Sparta, such as Hippias, the former tyrant of Athens, and Demaratus, the former king of Sparta, lived in the empire for a period, as well. Little is known about the contact between Indians and Greeks; Scylax's exploration of the Indus is the first record of contact between the two people. But there must have been regular commercial contacts in the main markets and palaces of the empire. Indians also served in Xerxes's army when he invaded Greece, and with Darius III against Alexander at Gaugamela.

Reconstruction of the Apadana at the Palace of Persepolis
(Image courtesy: Adobe Stock)

Philosophy and Religion: Persia, India and Greece

Around the time that the Persian Empire was established, unprecedented intellectual activity occurred in all parts of the then civilised world. It has become known as the Axial Age, a term coined by Karl Jaspers in his book *The Origin and Goal of History*. In Persia, Zoroaster endeavoured to purify the prevalent religion of polytheism, ritualism and magic; in Greece, there was a revolt against the traditional Homeric religion by the Ionian school that proposed a divine intelligence pervading and regulating the world; in Judea, a succession of Jewish religious reformers or 'prophets' appeared; in India, the authors of the Upanishads, dissatisfied with Vedic teaching, explored the nature of reality, and Buddha and Mahavira protested against the Vedas and the rituals and caste system of the priestly class; and in China, Confucius taught rational morality, while the legendary Lao Tzu described the Dao (the Way) as the source and ideal of all existence.

Zoroaster may have actually predated the Axial Age—estimates of his era range from the eleventh century BCE to the fifth century BCE. For him, the world was ruled by the two principles of Good (Ahura Mazda) and Evil (Ahriman). The struggle would be resolved by victory for Ahura Mazda, the dualism by monotheism. In his ethics, Zoroaster stressed good thoughts, words and deeds. He departed from Aryan polytheism and its rituals, forbidding bloody sacrifices and intoxicating drinks. The earlier Aryan 'devas' or gods, in his thought, became demons. Thus, Zoroaster's philosophy marks the dividing line between Iranian Aryans and Indian Aryans. 'Ahura' or 'asura' came to mean 'demon' in the Vedas.

Contact between the Iranian Aryans and Indian Aryans, who migrated gradually, was likely continuous, but it is not recorded. The earliest evidence of direct contact is from the Persian Empire. Ancient Indians concentrated on philosophies more than individual philosophers. The oldest philosophical tradition in India, and probably the world, is in the Vedas, but the Upanishads (900–600 BCE) contain its most brilliant exposition. In the Vedas, worship of half-personified powers of nature (fire, wind, rain) evolved into conceiving of the One, an underlying unity. This ultimate unity was systematically developed in the Upanishads toward monism. The true goal of life became liberation from the cycle of rebirths. Knowledge was exalted above works as a means of realising truth; the highest wisdom was self-realisation, or pure awareness.

Aspects of Indian philosophy were paralleled among Greek philosophers. The commonalities between Pythagoras (582–506 BCE) and Indian philosophy are striking. Singhal writes that: 'There is a far closer agreement between Pythagoras and the Indian doctrine, not merely in their general features, but even in certain details such as vegetarianism, and it may be added that the formulae which summarise the whole creed of "cycle and wheel" of births are likewise the same in both.'[4] Indeed, almost all the philosophical and mathematical doctrines ascribed to Pythagoras were known in India in the sixth century BCE. Pythagoras created an organised celibate brotherhood, which exercised very wide influence on religion, politics and the economy. Plato (427–347 BCE) greatly admired the Pythagorean School.

Indian Religions

By the fourth century BCE, Brahmanism in India had developed into a complex religious system. Vedic rituals persisted, albeit adjusted to contemporary needs. Brahmans regarded themselves as God's elect and had begun to enjoy a dominant position in society, with a measure of temporal power. Their religion involved expensive and cumbersome rituals as well as bloody sacrifice, though its practice was restricted to priests, aristocrats and the wealthy commercial community. People sought better paths to salvation. Drawing from philosophical speculation with roots in the *Rig Veda*, many sects emerged, each seeking an explanation of the universe: the most important were the Buddhists, Jains, Ajivikas and Nirgranthas. Doctrinal differences were hotly debated.

Jainism, Ajivika and Buddhism originated around the Indian kingdom of Magadha. Both Buddha and Mahavira built on the doctrines of earlier prophets. Mahavira was the son of a Lichchhavi noble from the city of Vaishali; he started his career by joining the ascetics called Nirgranthas, but became dissatisfied. At the age of about forty, he started out on his own.

He preached for his thirty remaining years and established a religious order. When he died in Pava, he had 14,000 adherents. Related through his mother to several reigning kings, he had also gained official patronage.

The Ajivika sect was founded by Gosala, a colleague of Mahavira. His philosophy did not accept the concept of karma and held that all events were completely determined by cosmic principles over which there was no control—a denial, in effect, of free will. He had a large following, including Ashoka's mother, and possibly his father as well.

Buddha's career was similar to Mahavira's. He was the son of a noble Sakya of the city of Kapilavastu. After deciding that asceticism was not sufficient to achieve salvation, he preached the 'middle way' based on rational thought until he died at eighty at Kusinagara. He established the Buddhist Sangha, a network of proselytising monks and nuns that led to missionary expansion.

Buddha and Mahavira were both reformers of Brahmanism. They rejected the authority of the Vedas and opposed ritual animal sacrifice. Their followers were not, however, asked to give up their belief in Brahman gods. Buddhism may have begun as a revolt against the priesthood's domination, but it grew into a rebellion against social privilege and hierarchy. Buddha's order was open to all castes and received wide social support, including from kings. Despite consistent opposition from Brahmans, Buddhism evolved from a body of dissident views and breakthrough teachings into an independent religion.

As a religion, it was also easily understood by unsophisticated people and offered a workable solution to the problems of life. The 'middle way' did not require an understanding of metaphysics or asceticism. Importantly, it made no demands for expensive rituals. It enthroned reason in the place of revelation and made man his own maker. If thoughts and actions were pure, there was no need to make offerings to the gods. Buddha concentrated on individuals, not social hierarchy. Ethical behaviour, not lineage, determined a person's worth. Within the Sangha, spiritual achievement was open to all.

Alexander, Persia and India

By the fourth century BCE, the Persian Empire still officially included Hindush. But Persia did not control the region, which had split into independent kingdoms and tribes. After Alexander defeated Darius III in 330 BCE, he proclaimed himself Great King. In that capacity, he set out in 326 BCE to reclaim Bactria and Hindush. Some kings, such as Ambhi, the raja of Taxila, surrendered to Alexander upon his arrival; others gave battle, notably Paurava, who proved to be a worthy opponent. Alexander's panache and battle-tested army, and heavy rain that mired Paurava's war chariots in mud, helped the aggressor to prevail. Some historians rate this encounter as Alexander's greatest strategic battle.

During his sojourn in Hindush, Alexander and his retinue (which included philosophers, historians and educated officers) also found time for discussions with local philosophers. But when he attempted to push farther than Hindush, toward the eastern ocean, his troops mutinied. He was forced to return to Babylon by sailing down the Indus and marching across the Gedrosian Desert, reaching his destination about 324 BCE.

Chandragupta, Chanakya and Bindusara

No sooner had Alexander departed than his satraps (provincial governors) in Hindush began to be murdered. Within a few years, no Hellene remained in authority there. Alexander had divided the region into six satrapies, three on the west of the Indus and three on the east. The satraps on the west were Hellenes and Persians (Peithon, Oxyartes and Nicanor, and his successor, Phillip), and on the east, local rulers (Ambhi of Taxila, Paurava and Abhisares of Kashmir). Nicanor was the first to be assassinated. Phillip was sent to replace him, but his own mercenaries murdered him in 325 BCE, and the territory was ceded to Ambhi. After Alexander's death in 323 BCE, chaos prevailed in the empire as his generals began to fight for control. Peithon, the remaining Hellene in authority in Hindush, left in 321 BCE to join that struggle.

Amazingly, within a few years of Alexander's departure, Hindush came under the rule of Chandragupta, an obscure young man. (Plutarch records that a young Chandragupta met Alexander as he prepared to leave Hindush).[5] Chandragupta soon conquered the main kingdom to the east as well, unseating Dhana Nanda and established the Mauryan dynasty, which ruled a vast territory for about 140 years.

How did a young man, probably in his mid-twenties, manage this feat in little more than two years? Unfortunately, the details are as obscure as Chandragupta's origins. One plausible story begins with Chanakya, a learned Brahman who lived from 350 to 275 BCE, and to whom the royal governing manual, the *Arthasastra,* was much later attributed. His early life was spent mostly in Taxila, which was a centre of learning. As a young adult in pursuit of knowledge, he came east to Pataliputra, the capital of Magadha. Dhana Nanda had established a charity there, which Chanakya was chosen to manage. Soon thereafter, however, Dhana Nanda dismissed him, supposedly because of his poor manners.[6]

En route back to Taxila, Chanakya found the boy Chandragupta playing kings and court, a game for children. Some accounts suggest Chandragupta was the son of the last Nanda king by a lowborn woman. Buddhist tradition states that he was a member of the Moriyas of Pipphalivana and recipient of some of Buddha's ashes. Chanakya was so impressed by Chandragupta's potential that he purchased him from his foster father and took him to Taxila, where the boy was educated for seven or eight years under Chanakya's tutelage.

Chandragupta probably became militarily active around 324 BCE, in the Taxila area. Despite the existence of powerful local rulers such as Ambhi and Paurava, he managed to annex Alexander's territories. One source suggests that he recruited his army from the Punjab and made an alliance with a Himalayan chief, possibly Paurava. He then turned his attention to attacking Dhana Nanda, who was hated by his citizens. It was an ambitious undertaking, as Nanda was thought to have an army of 200,000 infantry, 20,000 cavalry, 2,000 chariots and 3,000 elephants.

Chandragupta gathered republican and monarchical tribes and marched on Magadha, but he was defeated. He regrouped in the Punjab and made attacks on the edges of the empire, before moving again against its centre. He succeeded on his second attempt, putting Dhana Nanda to the sword. Chanakya anointed Chandragupta as emperor around 321 BCE and served as his chief minister.

Magadha, approximately the modern state of Bihar, was the main centre of power, learning and culture in India for about a thousand years. Its period ran from the sixth century BCE through the fifth century CE, beginning with the Haryanka dynasty, followed by the Shishunaga, Nanda, Maurya and finally the Gupta dynasties. The area had two great Buddhist universities in Nalanda and Vikramashila, among the oldest centres of learning in India and in the world.

Nalanda was destroyed toward the end of the twelfth century. In its heyday, it attracted 10,000 students and 2,000 teachers from all over Asia, Turkey to Japan. The Chinese monk Xuanzang spent a couple of years studying and teaching there in the seventh century. The university was an architectural masterwork with eight compounds, ten temples and meditation halls. Courses offered included religion, history, law, medicine, public health, linguistics, architecture and astronomy.

(Modern Bihar suffered through a long period of very poor governance, scoring lowest in human development among the major states of India.[7] Almost eighty per cent of its population of about 105 million lives in poverty. A change in government in 2005 began to turn around its fortunes and its performance has improved. When I visited after the rains in 2004, the densely cultivated farms in the seventy miles between Patna and Bodh Gaya, where the Buddha experienced enlightenment, were lush, deep green with flourishing crops. The land has fertile alluvial soil and is well-irrigated by several rivers and abundant rainfall during the monsoon season.)

In the following years, Chandragupta moved south to consolidate his grip on the subcontinent. By 311 BCE, his empire included central India. Meanwhile, Seleucus Nicator, one of Alexander's generals, had secured his rule over Babylon and started a campaign to subdue the eastern territories that Alexander had overrun. He recovered Bactria with difficulty, but failed to make much headway in Hindush. A treaty concluded his confrontation with Chandragupta in 303 BCE;

in it, Seleucus ceded Afghanistan and Baluchistan in return for five hundred war elephants. The two rulers also entered into a *jus conubii,* exchanging daughters in marriage. Envoys travelled back and forth, and powerful aphrodisiacs were sent from India as well.

Megasthenes—Seleucus's ambassador—lived in Pataliputra from about 303 to 300 BCE. He recorded the sojourn in his *Indica,* a major source of information about the Mauryas. At the time, Pataliputra was the largest city in the world, about twice the size of Rome.[8] King Ajatashatru (493–462 BCE) had converted the original settlement into a fortified town and his successor King Udayin made it Magadha's capital fifty years later. Situated at the confluence of the Son and Ganges rivers, it was about nine miles long and 1.5 miles wide, encircled by a moat sixty feet deep. Beyond the moat was a massive timber palisade protecting the city, with sixty-four gates and 570 towers. The imperial palace was at the city's centre, surrounded by a park with fountains and fish ponds. According to Megasthenes: 'The ground plan is much the same as that of Persepolis. The central hall at Persepolis has an alignment of a hundred pillars and the one at Pataliputra has eighty pillars. A mason's mark on one of the stones at Pataliputra is remarkably similar to those found at Persepolis, suggesting a common source of the craftsmen.'[9] Persian craftsmen, who dispersed after Alexander's conquest, probably worked on building the palace. It had walls made of stone, that must have been collected by genii and carvings and sculptures that ornament windows are such that this age could not make.[10] Its pillars were gilded with gold vines and silver birds and inside were thrones, chairs of state, great vessels of gold, silver and copper studded with precious stones.[11] As emperor, Chandragupta lived in high style.

Reconstruction of the palace at Persepolis
(Image courtesy: Adobe Stock)

Sadly, almost nothing remains of the magnificent palace. Today, a visitor will find only a damaged section of a stone pillar displayed in an enclosure, a couple of muddy ponds with floating green vegetation and well-tended gardens with brick paths in an area cordoned off by the Archaeological Survey of India. Other pillar remnants have been excavated, but they are not kept at the site. Modern Patna is a sprawling, messy, chaotic city of 1.7 million people, with congested streets lined with stalls and shops. Only drivers familiar with Indian traffic conditions can navigate it. The highlight of my visit was the museum, which houses stone sculptures from the Mauryan and later Gupta periods.

Despite a large population, including many foreigners, crime was rare in Pataliputra in Chandragupta's time. Megasthenes reported that inhabitants had abundant means of subsistence, exceeded ordinary stature and were distinguished by their proud bearing. The rich citizens dressed gaily in flowered muslin embroidered with jewels; attendants carried umbrellas for nobles when they went into the road. Poorer people wore fillets (headbands) or turbans and robes of pure-white muslin or linen. The soil nearby bore all kinds of fruits and held great amounts of gold, silver, copper, iron and other metals, as well.

Chandragupta was a stern despot, enforcing strict order through an organised bureaucracy reaching all the way to the village level. He had an appointed and carefully vetted council of ministers; a huge standing army of as many as 600,000 infantry, 30,000 cavalry and 9,000 elephants; and an elaborate espionage system serving as the king's eyes and ears, an idea borrowed from the Persian kings. The empire was divided into four viceroyalties, with princes as viceroys (officials ruling in the name of the king, with regal authority), each assisted by another appointed council of ministers, which reported directly to the king rather than the viceroy. Provincial governors served under the viceroys.

Each level of government had its civil service and department heads, with periodic inspections by senior officials designed to prevent abuse of power. The administration concentrated on collecting revenue, managing public works and adjudicating disputes. As the empire expanded, the metropolitan administrative system was replicated in other areas, such as provincial capitals and major trade centres. But with poor roads and low levels of literacy, management probably remained much looser beyond the metropolitan areas.

Chandragupta ruled for twenty-four years before abdicating or disappearing. One version of his last years has it that he converted to Jainism after turning fifty, possibly after a twelve-year-long famine that ended in 300 BCE, and retired with Bhadrabahu, a Jaina saint, to Sravana Belgola in Mysore. There he is said to have died by slow starvation over the course of about twelve years. Another version suggests that it was Ashoka's grandson (Samprati Chandragupta) who abdicated and went south with Bhadrabahu, leaving a mystery regarding Chandragupta's earlier disappearance.[12]

Chandragupta's successor was his son Bindusara, who was said to have spotted skin. Hellenic sources know him as Amritaghata, a slayer of foes. He conquered sixteen states in the subcontinent and seems to have extended the empire to the south. He received Deimachos as envoy from Antiochos I (King of Syria) and Dionysius from Ptolemy II Philadelphus (King of Egypt). Bindusara wrote to Antiochos asking for sweet wine, dried figs and a sophist (a Greek teacher of philosophy and other subjects). He may have followed the Ajivika religion. The names of three sons are recorded as his potential successors: Sushima, the eldest; Ashoka; and his brother Vitashoka. Legend suggests that Bindusara had 101 sons from 16 wives. He died after nearly thirty years in power, around 272 BCE.

CHAPTER 5

Ashoka

Childhood and Youth[1]

A shoka was born around 300 BCE. A prominent legend claims that he was ugly, with rough skin that was unpleasant to see and touch, and for that reason his father disliked him. An image of Ashoka sculpted on a panel of the South Gateway at the Sanchi Stupa in Madhya Pradesh shows him to be short, with a large round head and a paunch. British author Charles Allen speculates that the sculptor could not have seen him, because the gateway was erected about a century after the end of the Mauryan dynasty. But in all likelihood, memories of Ashoka still existed in the area, so the image could reflect his actual appearance.[2] It is also possible that the sculptor's skill was simply deficient, as the women surrounding Ashoka don't exactly look alluring. Nevertheless, partly based on how he looks on this panel, Dr Wig and S. Sharma in a 2015 issue of *The Indian Journal of Psychiatry* diagnose Ashoka as having suffered from Neurofibromatosis Type 1 or von Recklinghausen's disease, characterised by cutaneous (skin) neurofibromas and pigmented lesions called café-au-lait spots. They do not draw any psychological inferences from this diagnosis; surely, though, an ungainly appearance and rejection by his father must have affected Ashoka's development and character.

Mural depicting Emperor Ashoka fainting into the arms of his queens at the sight of the dying Bodhi Tree, with attendants bearing jugs of milk to restore the tree to health (*Image courtesy: Deepika Rajjak*)

Other historians also mention that Ashoka was unattractive. Although there is no mention of his ungainly appearance in his edicts, the idea is widely accepted probably because other legends support it—in one, in an earlier life, Ashoka gave Buddha dirt as a gift (it was all he had), which transformed into rough skin when he was reincarnated. And Bindusara's spotted skin, mentioned in other legends, could also have been passed on to his son.

Research by Dr I. Elia describes the skewed treatment received by unattractive children and the impact on their development: 'At least fifteen studies have shown that mothers treat attractive children more favourably than unattractive ones, even though they say they don't and may actually believe that. At least one of these studies showed this bias is true from birth.... Even as children, according to thirty-three separate studies, the attractive are better adjusted and more popular than the ugly.'[3] Adding to that, Dr E. Ritvo, a psychiatrist and author, has shown that skin conditions in particular have a profound effect on social behaviour and opportunity. And according to a meta-analysis by A. Khaleque and R.P. Rohner of thirty-six studies involving 10,000 participants, rejection by a father who has much greater prestige than the mother can deeply affect a boy's development, causing considerable emotional pain, anxiety and insecurity, damaging his self-image. This effect holds regardless of race and culture.

John Strong relates a story from the *Asokavadana* in which Ashoka's father—King Bindusara—decides to test his sons to determine the best successor. Bindusara asks Pingalavatsajiva, a wandering ascetic, to examine them. When Ashoka's mother asks him to join the other princes at the Garden of the Golden Pavilion, Ashoka at first retorts, 'Why should I [go]? The very sight of me is hateful to the King.'[4] After the interview, Pingalavatsajiva concludes that Ashoka will ascend the throne and tells his mother. She responds by urging the ascetic to go into exile. Bindusara dislikes Ashoka's looks, she says, and thus would also dislike the ascetic's appraisal.

One source mentions that Ashoka's mother's name was Subhadrangi,[5] and that she was the beautiful daughter of a Brahman. A prophecy declared that she was to be the mother of two sons—one a universal monarch and the other a recluse. The Brahman, seeking to fulfil the prophecy, managed to introduce his daughter into the palace. At the time, kings had several queens and a harem. Because the other queens and ladies in Bindusara's harem were jealous of Subhadrangi's beauty, she was initially given the menial duties of a barber but, in time, the king noticed her, took her into his favour and eventually made her the chief queen. When she finally bore him a son, she chose the name Ashoka (which means 'without sorrow'). Having a male child, an heir to the throne, elevated her status, so she loved the boy despite his appearance. When she bore Bindusara a second son, she named him Vitashoka ('sorrow terminated').

Berkeley psychologist Linda Druschel, in a personal conversation, observed that 'Ashoka obviously developed into a remarkable human being who was capable of profound compassion. One can only imagine that whatever deficits he experienced because of his rejection by his father and due to his appearance were compensated for by the presence, active nurturing and loving regard provided by his mother. That is probably the key piece in his developmental puzzle.'

In the absence of real evidence on Ashoka as a person, of course, it is not possible to draw anything like a complete profile of his character and its development. All that history has provided are stories written centuries later, by authors who surely had their own agendas. What we can do, though, is paint a credible picture from the legends that does not contradict the inscriptions. As interesting as our speculations may be, it is important to bear in mind that Ashoka's character as expressed in his edicts is the only real evidence of his existence at present and must be given by far the most credence.

As a younger junior prince with an unattractive appearance, we can suspect that he was teased mercilessly. Heaped on top of rejection by his father, this treatment would have made him shy, introspective and, perhaps, insecure, but inclined to work hard to compensate for his perceived disadvantage—a drive he may have inherited from his father and grandfather. He might have tried to develop a pleasing personality to win the approval of his peers and elders. Because of his mother's affection for him and her devotion to religion, Ashoka might have depended on the emotional support of women and the consolation of religion, later in his life, as well. Charles Allen contends that he might have exhibited wrathful tendencies at an early age that later earned him the title of Chandashoka ('fierce or cruel'),[6] although no legend supports this view of his behaviour before he ascended to the throne.[7]

On a positive note, as an ugly person, Ashoka was in the company of renowned philosophers: Jean Paul Sartre considered his ugliness to count as a disability; and Socrates made a big deal of his ugliness, leading academic and author Andy Martin to conclude that dissatisfaction with one's own appearance is an engine of philosophy.[8] Perhaps Ashoka's physical appearance contributed to his philosophical and social bent.

In any case, when Ashoka was young, he had a slim chance of becoming king. For one thing, he had an elder half-brother who was the crown prince. For another, his father found him repulsive. Though unloved, he was still a prince who had the run of the era's most magnificent palace—not a bad place to spend a childhood.

After having mastered basic instruction, princes were taught political economy, philosophy, diplomacy, war strategy and the use of weapons. Ashoka's teachers were men of reputation in their fields, with both theoretical and practical knowledge, including ministers of state, academics, philosophers and generals. One of them could have been Chanakya, a consummate philosopher, strategist and administrator. Another was likely Radhagupta, who later helped Ashoka ascend the throne and served as his chief minister. Ashoka was probably in attendance when foreign ambassadors came to court, as well, exposing him to ideas from other cultures.

The exchange of ideas under the Persian Empire had pushed philosophers from Greece, Egypt, Mesopotamia, Persia and India to question existing philosophical systems. This global ferment surely fed into Ashoka's learning. Partly to compensate for his disability, he was likely an avid student and must have excelled at school. By the age of eighteen, he was considered the most capable prince, and his father, perhaps at Radhagupta's urging, sent him to Taxila to resolve a citizens' revolt against the province's ministers. His elder brother, the Crown Prince Sushima, was serving as viceroy there, but he had failed to settle the politically sensitive problem. Ashoka succeeded in resolving the revolt without violence. His actions exhibited a compassionate, benevolent and benign attitude,[9] suggesting that he had an agile mind and the political skill to address a delicate and dangerous situation without the use of force. His success may also have sparked his brother's jealousy.

About twenty miles from Islamabad in Pakistan, Taxila is now a UNESCO World Heritage Site. Not much can be seen beyond foundation lines, but a nearby museum houses some stunning Gandharan Buddhist stucco sculpture. In Ashoka's time, Taxila was the junction of three great trade routes to Persia and Western Asia; to Central Asia and China; and to Magadha. The university at Taxila was renowned as a centre for learning, especially for mathematics, astronomy, medicine, Sanskrit and grammar. The Dharmarajika stupa at the site is ascribed to Ashoka and is thought to have been built later in his reign.

Ashoka's successful resolution of the Taxila revolt finally won him his father's favour, and he was appointed the viceroy of Avanti province. Ujjain, its capital, was even then an old, established and holy city. Hindu legend has it that Lord Krishna was educated in Ujjain by his guru, and that the city was one of the four places where drops of the nectar of immortality fell. For that reason, it is one of the sites of the Kumbh Mela pilgrimage, which takes place every twelve years and attracts millions of people who come to take a dip in the Shipra River. Ujjain has been home to notable scholars and to Kalidasa, a giant of ancient Indian literature. The city was also considered the prime meridian by Hindu astrologers starting in the fourth century BCE, and was placed at the centre of the world in ancient maps. Today, it has about half a million inhabitants, small for a city in India and is considered dull, except for its many temples.

Viceroy

Ashoka was viceroy of Avanti province for about ten years. Avanti contained a large part of central India, north of the Vindhya Range. It was known for commerce and agriculture, especially wheat. The journey to Ujjain, from either Taxila or Pataliputra, was around a thousand miles, a very long trip in that era. Ashoka must have travelled in a horse-drawn chariot, with a retinue of attendants and an armed guard. From Taxila, the route probably ran along the main north-to-east arterial route through Punjab and Rajasthan, before turning south on a trade route to Vidisha and Ujjain. From Pataliputra, he would have taken the same arterial route in the other direction and turned south west from the middle Gangetic plains over the Vindhyan highlands to Vidisha.[10]

Avanti had two important Buddhist centres, in Vidisha and Sanchi. At the time of Ashoka's arrival, Vidisha had been an established trading centre for two or three centuries. It was known for producing sharp-edged swords, weaving and ivory carving. Ancient inscriptions found in the area record gifts by a banker, a banker's wife, a weaver, a labourer and an ivory worker. Rich in ancient monuments, some dating as far back as 140 BCE (but none from the Mauryan period), modern Vidisha is a shabby, dusty town with narrow lanes and 150,000 inhabitants. Its small museum houses sculptures from the ninth century CE onward, attesting to the region's unbroken artistic activity.

The stupas at Sanchi are a UNESCO World Heritage Site,[11] and among the most important historical places of Buddhist pilgrimage. Surprisingly, when I went, I was the sole visitor. Even the office was closed. I was able to wander the site in solitude, look at the carvings at leisure and absorb the ambiance of Ashoka's history. Whenever I visit such places, I feel humbled and deeply aware of his great effort to persuade his administration to provide good governance, and his citizens to follow the ethical path he advocated. In my work, I have glimpsed how difficult this sort of persuasion is, even for a short period in a small area. Astonishingly, Ashoka attempted it for three decades, on a sub-continental scale.

The main stupa is among the oldest surviving stone structures in India. The magnificent stupa at Sanchi is attributed to Ashoka, but it was likely built after his time. Its core was a hemispherical structure built over Buddha's relics. Ashoka is said to have retrieved these relics and distributed them widely, building stupas over them in each case. Later rulers embellished Ashoka's stupa with sculpted gateways and railings, many depicting scenes from Buddha's and Ashoka's lives, and built other stupas nearby. The panel discussed earlier, showing Ashoka's distress at seeing damage to the Bodhi Tree, can be found here. Ashoka also built a stone pillar at Sanchi inscribed with an edict exhorting the Buddhist Sangha to remain united.

Sanchi Stupa *(Photo courtesy: Adobe Stock)*

In Vidisha, just 150 miles from Ujjain, Ashoka met and fell in love with Devi, the beautiful daughter of a prominent local merchant. No record of a marriage exists, but they cohabited for about ten years. In the hamlet of Panguraria (about forty-five miles from Vidisha) is this inscription on a rock: 'The king [now after consecration] is called Piyadasi [once],[12] came to this place on a pleasure tour while he was still a [ruling] prince, living together with his unwedded consort.'[13] Devi bore him two children—Mahinda and Sanghamitta. Another inscription tells a similar story: 'Ashoka made her [Devi] his wife and she was [afterward] with child by him and bore in Ujjain a beautiful boy, Mahinda, and when two years had passed [she bore] a daughter, Sanghamitta.'

Ashoka's relationship with Devi was unusual for any era: He was a prince and she a commoner, from a commercial caste. Even though Ashoka's grandfather Chandragupta was of humble origin, by his generation the dynasty must have become firmly established in the ruling caste.[14] Applying modern perspective to personal relationships thousands of years ago is obviously highly speculative, but some basic human connections remain timeless, whatever social norms may be. Breaking those norms implies that Ashoka and Devi shared a strong attraction— likely more than just physical, given his appearance. (It's true, of course, that his royalty could have attracted her and her beauty attracted him). Devi could have also provided the emotional support he needed, in the absence of his mother's affection, while he worked to master his newfound political and administrative responsibilities.

As Devi was a devout Buddhist, it is likely that Ashoka either already shared her religion's core values or came to share them while they cohabited. Their shared beliefs may have cemented their relationship. Given that Ashoka was from a formerly lower-caste family that had achieved greatness, Buddhism's emphasis on individual endeavour must have appealed to him. Having to rely on his own effort to overcome his disability—and later, command respect—could have reinforced that appeal. Buddha's non-theist, intellectual approach to addressing life's issues must also have been attractive to the intelligent, introspective man that he was.

Ashoka's years in Avanti gave him the opportunity to learn how to manage a well-established bureaucracy and administer a prosperous region, while maintaining good relations with his father and his ministers at the capital. He matured, started a family and diligently gained mastery of the job he expected to do for the rest of his life. When he, instead, became emperor and left for the capital, Devi remained in Vidisha. History does not record whether it was her decision or Ashoka's.

Emperor

Bindusara died in 272 BCE. Sushima, Ashoka's elder brother and crown prince, was expected to succeed their father; instead, the throne was vacant for four years. What happened in that interregnum is the stuff of speculation.

Several conflicting and confusing legends exist, all of which agree on a struggle for the throne. One source claims that when Bindusara was dying, he wished to appoint the Crown Prince Sushima as king, but his ministers placed Ashoka on the throne instead. Another source adds to the story, claiming that Sushima offended Bindusara's chief minister, who then conspired to exclude him from the throne by sending him to manage another revolt in Taxila just as Bindusara was falling ill. Bindusara attempted to recall Sushima and send Ashoka in his place, but his ministers prevented the switch. After Bindusara died, Sushima marched against Ashoka to assert his right to the crown. Radhagupta, Ashoka's supporter and future chief minister, tricked the prince with an image of Ashoka atop an elephant that was surrounded by a ditch of burning charcoal; Sushima charged the image and fell into the ditch, where he perished. Yet another legend has Ashoka in Taxila when his father died; despite the distance from the capital, in this telling, he was able to seize the throne with Radhagupta's help.

Authors Charles Allen and Sanjeev Sanyal contend that when Bindusara died, Sushima was away in the Northwest frontier fending off incursions. Ashoka, they say, took control of Pataliputra with the help of Greek mercenaries he got to know a decade earlier, during his brief sojourn in Taxila. Ashoka and the mercenaries later defeated Sushima, who came to claim the throne with the Mauryan army. Does this speculation make sense? The Greek settlements were in modern North Pakistan and Afghanistan, and Ashoka was either still in

Ujjain as viceroy, or had already travelled to Pataliputra at the time of his father's death. The mercenaries would have had to either come to Ujjain (a trip of about 850 miles) and march with Ashoka to Pataliputra, 750 miles away, or meet him there directly (a 1,245-mile trip). Meanwhile, Sushima was in Taxila, about 930 miles from Pataliputra. Just looking at the distances involved, it seems implausible that the mercenaries could have beaten the rightful heir to the capital.

Even if Ashoka did reach Pataliputra ahead of his brother, the Mauryan army stationed there would have confronted him. This army was about 600,000 strong, according to legend, and had not lost a battle for about fifty years under Chandragupta and Bindusara. It had fought Seleucus, an experienced Macedonian general, to a draw, if not outright defeat. Even if a quarter of that force was guarding the capital, is it credible that Ashoka, who had never before commanded an army in battle, could have gathered enough mercenaries to defeat it? And, when Sushima returned, presumably with the support of the remaining Mauryan army, is it credible that the same band of mercenaries defeated him? Ashoka could not have conquered Pataliputra and defended it against Sushima without massive defections and support from the Mauryan army.

With his Buddhist leanings and Devi at his side, Ashoka was likely reluctant to challenge his brother for the throne; it would have been a very risky move and he had a family to consider. If the challenge failed, none of them would have survived. His elevation may have been a gradual political manoeuvre devised with Radhagupta, developed over three or four years to raise the probability of a successful challenge for the good of the empire, which they may have feared Sushima was not prepared to manage. Perhaps Sushima was at first allowed to rule, but his father's ministers withheld their approval pending evidence of his ability to govern. When he displayed his incompetence,

Radhagupta persuaded Ashoka to challenge him by assuring him of the army's support.

However, he obtained the throne, many legends agree that Ashoka's cruel behaviour began just after his ascension. The new king is said to have been responsible for the death of not just Sushima, but his other brothers as well—from six to as many as ninety-nine, in all. John Strong quotes passages from the *Asokavadana* describing a torture chamber where hundreds were put to death while Ashoka consolidated his grip on the empire; absurd orders were given to his ministers and the 500 who did not obey were decapitated; 500 women in his harem were burned to death because they disliked caressing him.

As hard as it is to square these accounts with earlier descriptions of a gentle, pious Ashoka, it's possible that to fulfil his ambition and prove himself worthy, he acquiesced to Radhagupta's influence and actions to consolidate his position. But the obvious exaggeration of the numbers tests the credibility of the stories and legends that include the slaughter of nearly one hundred brothers (all but one, allegedly) are contradicted by evidence showing that some of Ashoka's brothers were still alive during his reign. If Ashoka were an aggressive and cruel usurper, surely he would have wanted to immediately prove his military prowess by conquering Kalinga, a weaker neighbouring kingdom, to bolster his claim to be the king. That he waited for eight years to make that move casts serious doubt on the conjecture that he was aggressive and wantonly cruel.

David Shulman, in his review of Upinder Singh's *Political Violence in India,* says that Buddhist tradition deliberately paints Ashoka as a sadistic megalomaniac before his conversion. Was his reign of terror made up to show the dramatic change in his persona after he became a Buddhist? Such climactic conversion stories are a staple of Buddhist hagiographies.

In any case, we can say with some confidence that Ashoka was crowned emperor around 269 BCE. The emperor-designate would have first visited his ministers' homes to obtain their formal consent; they could withhold their permission, as they may have done with Sushima, but seldom did. At the coronation, the prince would have sat on a throne covered with a tiger's skin and been sprinkled with water brought from different oceans and rivers in his realm. He would have repeated the coronation oath, vowing to rule his subjects according to the sacred laws. Afterward, in celebration, there would have been customary games and chariot races in the capital. Often, the new king released prisoners and commuted death sentences, which Ashoka continued to do on each anniversary of his coronation.

The chief queen for most of his long reign was Asandhimitta. In legend, she was a perfect wife and support for Ashoka, an emotional replacement for Devi and his mother. She was the mother of Kunala, who was said to have beautiful eyes. (One source mentions another wife, Padmavati, as the mother of Crown Prince Kunala, but this could simply have been another name for Asandhimitta.) A few years after her death, Tissarakha became the queen; she was responsible for damaging the Bodhi Tree and blinding Kunala. (Karuvaki, the mother of Prince Tivara, is mentioned in an edict as another queen; as with Asandhimitta/Padmavati, it is possible that she and Tissarakha were the same person.) Various texts mention four sons in all—Mahinda, Kunala, Tivara and Jalauka, although it's possible, once again, that some of these are substitute names for a single person. Ashoka had at least two daughters, Sanghamitta and Charumati. His grandsons include Samprati, son of Kunala, and Dasharatha, both of whom became his successors.

Little is recorded about the first eight years of Ashoka's reign. Some aspects of his life can be gleaned from his edicts—he was a vigorous ruler and spent much of his time administering the empire. He attended to urgent matters immediately and responded to petitions personally, dispatching business at all hours. He kept informed through a network of reporters, and a large and experienced bureaucracy served the empire, collecting taxes and maintaining law and order over millions of disparate people spread across a vast territory.

The Mauryas developed their centralised royal rule, which the Nandas had begun, into a vast empire that merged tribal states throughout most of central India. Ashoka ruled as a caring, attentive father, declaring in one edict that 'all people are my children.' He sought to maintain good order throughout the empire, promoting morality, fairness and compassion at all levels of his administration and among the citizenry at large. He governed not only through his bureaucrats but also through regular contact with his citizens, enabled by an elaborate reporting system as well as grand tours through many of the areas he controlled.

He was advised by a ministerial council, whose members he chose, but made the ultimate decisions regarding all imperial matters himself. A treasurer, working with the chief of tax collection, was responsible for the royal treasury and state income, which came from taxes on production and trade; most of that income was spent on salaries for government leaders (down to the administrators, judges, etc., in each region) and for the army, as well as for public works—roads, irrigation, rest houses, provision for people in need, etc.

As in Chandragupta's time, Ashoka's empire was divided into four major provinces. Taxila was the northern capital, Ujjain the western, Tosali the eastern and Suvarnagiri the southern. The council of ministers had more sway in provincial matters than in imperial concerns; they served as the most direct contact between the king and his viceroys, and sometimes incurred the wrath of citizens, such as in Taxila during Bindusara's reign, for meddling in local affairs.

High officials called *Mahamattas* served in the government, as well. They acted as ombudsmen, empowered to counter the abuse of power—the first such officials in India, and likely the world. Ashoka emphasised just behaviour and fair judgments, and cautioned his judges against laziness, fatigue and impatience that could wrongly affect rulings. To guard against judicial misconduct, he sent *Mahamattas* to inspect the legal system in each territory every five years; provincial *Mahamattas* carried out inspections every three years. Ashoka revoked the practice of meting out punishments by caste, and required that all people be treated equally under the law.

The administration had three levels: metropolitan, core areas and peripheral regions. Metropolitan areas were closely administered by their own hierarchies, but administration was looser in outlying areas. The core areas were connected by trade routes and were governed by a hierarchy of officials similar to the metropolitan administration at the upper levels, but less so at the local levels. The peripheral regions were loosely governed.

Cities had a hierarchical governing structure to deal with every kind of civil affair, including public safety. The empire's four provinces were divided into administrative districts, with layers of officials in each district. An overseer managed and monitored the provincial officials' work, and three such overseers could handle serious legal issues. Below them were officials who acted as judges and assessors in rural regions, adjudicating agricultural affairs and land disputes. Lower down were officials who handled accounting and secretarial duties, and collected taxes from small groups of villages. Individual villages had their own officials who handled local matters and reported to the next level above them.

Ashoka also appointed special *Mahamattas* to deal with frontier and indigenous people, to establish medical and veterinary centres, and to handle matters relating to women's welfare. There were officials in charge of irrigation and forestry; Ashoka insisted on prudent management of timber, forbidding clear cutting and burning to free up land. And there was, of course, a huge military administration to handle all aspects of managing hundreds of thousands of army troops, along with thousands of horses and elephants, armaments, etc.

There were also agents who handled public relations for the king in local areas, as well as the reporters who had direct access to the king, wherever he was. Under the Achaemenid Persians, from whom much of this administrative structure was likely inherited, such reporters were known as the king's eyes and ears, serving as a vital line of communication between the imperial and provincial administrations.

Every official of Ashoka's administration had to propagate Dhamma, especially concerning the treatment of slaves, servants, Brahmans, parents, old people, prisoners and animals. In the fourteenth year of his reign, Ashoka named powerful new officials, *Dhamma-Mahamattas*, specifically to promote Dhamma in all areas of life, religious and secular.

The whole system worked effectively, with a remarkable king who was totally engaged. The eventual downfall of the Mauryan Empire may well have been because of Ashoka's decline and disengagement toward the end of his life, and the inability of his successors to manage such a daunting administrative project.

Kalinga War

The first major recorded event of Ashoka's reign was the Kalinga War, in his ninth regnal year (about 260 BCE). The war may have been launched to put an end to border raids by the Kalingans, or simply to open land and sea routes to the south and east, facilitating trade within the subcontinent and with South East

Asia—conquest of territory was part of a ruler's job description in that era. Ashoka's grandfather had conquered a vast area, and his father had added sixteen territories to it. His Brahman and ministerial advisors may have sensed an opportunity for him to become a 'chakravartin raja' (universal ruler), an important objective for rulers in their philosophy. The concept originated in the Vedic era, but it was reinforced by the Persian Empire and by Ashoka's own ancestors.

Chakravartin bas-relief at Amaravati, the great Buddhist monument in India, depicting a wheel-turning ruler (looking somewhat like Ashoka) benignly governing according to *Dhamma (Image courtesy: Deepika Rajjak)*

Kalinga was a formidable kingdom. Ancient authors including Megasthenes and Pliny the Elder recognised its greatness; much later, in the seventh century CE, the Chinese Buddhist pilgrim Xuanzang made a visit. Kalinga reached its apex under the rule of Kharavela around the first century BCE, when Jainism flourished under his sponsorship. Its maritime trade extended all the way to Sumatra. Some of its traders settled in South East Asia, where they spread Buddhism, Hinduism, the Indian epics, architecture and engineering. Until recently, Indians in South East Asia were known as 'Kelings'.

The modern state of Odisha—the area that includes much of ancient Kalinga—remains rich in religious tradition, with some major Hindu temples as well as Buddhist and Jain pilgrimage sites. (Dhauli, the place of Ashoka's epiphany, is a Buddhist pilgrimage site because of the version of his edicts located there.) Bhubaneswar, its capital, is home to nearly a thousand temples. It is known for its arts and crafts, as well as ancient and traditional dance. The state has a long coastline and abundant natural resources, including coal and bauxite, but has not yet developed enough economically to lift the majority of its forty-two million people out of poverty. In 2006, sixty-three per cent of its population fell below the poverty line, placing it among the poorest states in India.[15]

It is notable that Ashoka waited eight years for his first conquest, especially as he commanded a huge army, superior to any in the subcontinent. He must have felt pressure to follow in his forefathers' more aggressive footsteps, especially from Radhagupta, who had helped him secure the throne. Perhaps he first tried diplomacy, to persuade Kalinga to accept Mauryan suzerainty without war. When that did not succeed, the pressure must have become strong enough to overcome his leanings toward non-violence. As a relatively young apprentice ruler, beholden to his ministers, he may not have had sufficient confidence to go against them when his initial approach was not successful. Perhaps his military advisors assured him that there would be few casualties because of the Mauryan army's overwhelming superiority. Megasthenes recorded Kalinga's forces as 60,000 foot soldiers, 700 war elephants and a 1,000 horsemen.[16] Although large, it was about one-tenth of the putative strength of the Mauryan army.

After many years of indecision, Ashoka approved the invasion. His remorse for this action is expressed in Edict XIII, presented in Chapter 2 and in the Appendix. The carnage of war caused him deep distress, and triggered a searing identity crisis. He resolved it by seeking refuge in religion, as many people faced with crises still do. In doing so he followed his mother's path, but chose the faith of Devi, the woman with whom he had spent his formative years—Buddhism. He had probably already absorbed the religion's precepts intellectually, but it was only now that he began to develop an emotional understanding of and commitment to the way of the Buddha.

It was a turning point in his emotional development, shifting his inclination from pleasing temporal beings such as his father and Radhagupta to pleasing a higher being, the Buddha. In a sense, he came into his own, confident of his values and direction. With effort, he gradually became an ardent Buddhist, committed to non-violence. It is possible that he even adopted the garb and practices of a monk, including meditation, for short periods. I-tsing, a traveller from China, 1,000 years after Ashoka's time, recorded seeing statues of him wearing a monk's robe. After his epiphany, Ashoka ruled his vast empire largely without violence. He became an evangelist, preaching Dhamma, his code of social ethics, throughout his realm and in foreign lands.

Buddhist

Historians agree that Ashoka was a Buddhist, but continue to debate the timing of his conversion. Was it before or after the Kalinga War? Was it gradual or sudden? Who or what was the catalyst for the change? Most agree that the sudden-conversion narrative is a somewhat self-serving Buddhist legend, especially as Ashoka is portrayed as cruel prior to his conversion.

Buddhism is not based on faith or revelation. It requires study, thought and practice. For that reason, discussions of Ashoka's 'conversion' as a single point in time are not useful. It's more likely that he became deeply committed to Buddhism only after Kalinga, as the consequences of that war sunk in. In the ensuing edicts, he provided ample evidence of his growing devotion to Buddha's teachings, and his commitment to living and spreading their essence.

He started with the Minor Rock Edict, dated just a few years after the Kalinga War. 'Thus speaks the Beloved-of-the-Gods Devanampiya Ashoka: I have been a Buddhist layman for more than two-and-a-half years, but for a year I did not make much progress. Now for more than a year, I have drawn closer to the Order and have become more ardent. The gods, who up to this time did not associate with men, now mingle with them, and this is the result of my efforts. Moreover, this is not something to be obtained only by the great, but it is also open to the humble, if they are earnest they can reach heaven easily. Both the humble and the great should make progress, and the neighbouring peoples also should know that the progress is lasting. And this investment will increase and increase abundantly, and increase by half as much again...'

He confirmed his commitment in Major Rock Edict VIII, written in response to a visit to the Bodhi Tree. In the *Asokavadana*, Ashoka declares that he has grasped the supreme essence and insight into who he is, by performing acts of merit. And in the Bhabra Rock Inscription, Ashoka addressed the Sangha (Buddhist community), suggesting texts that they should hear frequently and meditate upon. He donated generously to the Sangha, as well, sponsoring the Quinquennial Festival and personally serving food to monks.

Both Sanjeev Sanyal and David Shulman quote the *Asokavadana* to suggest that Ashoka continued to be cruel after he became an ardent Buddhist. He is supposed to have slaughtered thousands of Ajivikas and Jains for slights against the Buddha. They also point to a sentence from Rock Edict XIII, his expression of remorse after the Kalinga War, that offers a warning to the forest people to not take advantage of his restraint. These authors contend that if Ashoka could threaten the forest people, he could certainly have slaughtered thousands of Ajivikas and Jains. This is an absurd extrapolation. These religions were practiced by his mother and grandfather, respectively; to butcher people devoted to them would have been cultural anathema. As a skilled politician, he might have censured the offending Jains and Ajivikas as he did dissenting members of the Buddhist Sangha (see page 58) whose ideas may have posed a greater threat to his core beliefs, but willful slaughter is not credible.

Looking more broadly at all twenty-eight discovered edicts, rather than a single sentence of just one, we see that they consistently express compassion, non-violence, concern for citizens' welfare and Ashoka's devotion to Buddhism and the Sangha. But Sanyal says that Ashoka's devotion was not genuine—that it had more to do with politics of succession than anything else. If Ashoka had made his spiritual choice cynically, though, why would he choose Buddhism, a small sect, and not Brahmanism, which had the largest following?

What his critics suggest, essentially, is a split personality: an Ashoka who preached compassion in his edicts from the ages of about forty-two to fifty-eight, while sadistically butchering people at the same time. There have been leaders like this, such as Stalin, whose propaganda suggested that the USSR was a workers' paradise even as millions were being killed in purges or sent to rot in gulags. But there is clear evidence of Stalin's misdeeds. There is no evidence to suggest that Ashoka was cruel after he accepted Buddhism. Indeed, the only evidence available is from his edicts, which show him to be a non-violent and compassionate ruler. Until more support for them is found, the embellished legends of Ashoka's wanton cruelty should remain doubtful. Some scholars, such as John Strong, have noted that the mix of cruelty and compassion in the *Asokavadana* could also reflect the ongoing anxiety among Buddhists that secular rulers can go bad. In reality, of course, Buddhism probably would have remained an insignificant sect had it not benefited from Ashoka's support.

Inscription on Ashoka Pillar *(Image courtesy: Deepika Rajjak)*

Bodhi Tree
(Photo courtesy: Ashok Khanna)

Third Buddhist Council

Apparently, according to the Southern Tradition, the Buddhist Sangha's unity was threatened during Ashoka's rule, as many heretics had infiltrated the Order. This concerned Ashoka, who used his imperial office to issue a stern warning against schismatic activity. He ordered the expulsion of anyone disrupting the unity of the Sangha and asked his imperial officers to enforce his commands.

The Schism Edict at Sanchi says: 'The Beloved-of-the-Gods, orders the officers of Kausambi/Pataliputra thus: No one is to cause dissension in the Order. The Order of monks and nuns has been united, and this unity should last for as long as my sons and great grandsons and the moon and the sun. Whoever creates a schism, is to be dressed in white and put in a place not inhabited by monks and nuns. It is my wish that the Order remains united and endures for long. You must keep one copy of this document in your meeting hall and give one copy to the laity.'

The Third Buddhist Council was convened to mediate differing views. Evidence of this meeting is sketchy, though archaeological research indicates that a huge building, which could have accommodated the assembly, was built in ancient times just outside Pataliputra, and the gathering has tremendous importance in the Buddhist canon. Ashoka's edicts do not mention it directly, but the Schism Edict suggests his concern about a sectarian split. According to the Southern Tradition, the council was held during his nineteenth regnal year, around 250 BCE, 236 years after Buddha's death. It is possible that the process began then but ended about a decade later, when some definite criterion for judging an orthodox Buddhist had been established.

At the end of the Third Council, Moggaliputta Tissa, the council president, is believed to have composed 'Points of Controversy' and dispatched missions to many parts of India and beyond. Buddhist monks were reputedly sent as missionaries to Kashmir, Andhra, Mysore, Maharashtra, the Himalayan territories, Sri Lanka, and possibly modern Myanmar and Thailand. These missions were sent primarily to communicate the Third Council's decisions, but also to add converts. They were separate from Ashoka's ambassadorial and Dhamma missions, but the two efforts eventually converged, and Buddhism emerged as a religion with a mass following. Buddhist communities sprang up all over the Indian subcontinent, enjoying Ashoka's patronage. His support also provided the momentum that later made Buddhism a major world religion.

Linked with the Third Buddhist Council is the story of Ashoka's son Mahinda's mission to Sri Lanka. To show his friendship and respect, Tissa, king of Sri Lanka, had sent a mission to India headed by his nephew, Maha Arittha; Ashoka's court welcomed them, and they returned after a stay of five months, carrying Ashoka's message: 'I have taken refuge in Buddha, the law and order. I have avowed myself a lay disciple of the doctrine of the son of the Sakyas. Imbue your mind also with faith in this Triad, in the highest religion of the Jina; take refuge in the teacher.' Mahinda followed the mission a month later. His preaching persuaded Tissa to accept Buddha's teaching. The king then built Mahavihara, the first monastery in Sri Lanka, for Mahinda.

Soon afterward, Tissa's queen Anula, with 500 attendants, desired to enter the Order, as well. As male missionaries had no power to convert women, it was suggested that Ashoka's daughter Princess Sanghamitta might do the honours. King Tissa sent his nephew back to Ashoka to request his daughter's presence and a branch of the Bodhi Tree. Ashoka gave his consent and with much ceremony, severed a branch of the tree at Bodh Gaya.

Sanghamitta subsequently came to Sri Lanka to preach to the queen, bringing the holy branch with her. It was planted in the Mahamegha garden, which King Tissa dedicated to the Buddhist Order. That tree still survives and is allegedly the oldest authenticated tree in the world. It is a sacred place for Buddhists. The king erected a nunnery for Sanghamitta, who remained there until her death, in 203 BCE. A stupa commemorating her life still exists.

Sri Lanka remains overwhelmingly Buddhist and is the main repository of the Theravada Tradition. Anuradhapura, a UNESCO World Heritage Site, was Sri Lanka's capital from the fourth century BCE to the eleventh century CE. It is situated about a four-hour drive north of Colombo, the capital. Within its sixteen-square mile area lie historical ruins and modern monasteries, including the one commemorating Sanghamitta.

The most famous monastery is the Brazen Palace, erected in 164 BCE. Once nine stories tall, only 1,600 stone pillars can be seen today. There is also a large stupa, known as a 'dagoba', which stands 400 feet high. It is the third tallest structure in the ancient world, just after the pyramids at Giza. I found the moonstones particularly fascinating—semi-circular carvings at the entrance to the monasteries, representing the transition from the secular to the sacred world traced by Buddha's path to enlightenment.

Tours

The Minor Rock Edict cited earlier is dated to about two years after the Kalinga War—Ashoka's tenth regnal year. He issued it while on his first 'Dhamma Yatra', or tour of piety, a pilgrimage spanning at least 256 days that he recorded in Rock Edict VIII. Among other places, he visited Bodh Gaya to pay homage to the Bodhi Tree. According to one Chinese traveller, Ashoka built the first shrine there, although no trace of that structure exists. In the fifteenth year of his reign, he enlarged for the second time a stupa for a Buddha (Konagamana) who lived before Gautama Buddha.[17]

Bodh Gaya is the most important Buddhist pilgrimage site. Surrounding the Mahabodhi Temple, where the Bodhi Tree is located, are monasteries built by a number of different countries and Buddhist traditions. A mess of stalls offering tourist kitsch mars the entrance to the temple. When I visited in 2004, a guide assured me that the commerce would be relocated soon, because the temple had been declared a UNESCO World Heritage Site, which requires easy and clear access.

The temple was built in the eleventh century, over the original one thought to be built by Ashoka and restored in the nineteenth century. During my visit, it was teeming with Buddhist pilgrims from all over the world. Nevertheless, a sense of calm and peace prevailed. Most of the chanting and meditation was near the Bodhi Tree. It is not the original tree, which died; luckily, the sapling taken by Ashoka's daughter to Sri Lanka became the source for the huge tree that now stands by the temple.

In his twentieth regnal year—a few months after an eclipse that occurred in 249 BCE—Ashoka visited Lumbini, Gautama Buddha's birthplace, in the foothills of the Himalayas. Gautama's mother Maya Devi was passing through on her way to her parents' home when she gave birth. The main historic item of interest there today is the Maya Devi Temple, parts of which date back to the third century BCE, and were perhaps originally built by Ashoka. But the site also has remains of monasteries from later eras, up to the fifth century CE, and stupas from as recently as the fifteenth century CE.

These ruins are not the largest part of the Lumbini complex, which is now a religious theme park. South East Asian countries have built the Theravada monasteries lining the east side; the west side has Mahayana monasteries built by countries that follow the Northern Tradition. Normally, I would have walked around and explored the various buildings, but it was raining when I visited the area, so I drove through, stopping at places that looked architecturally interesting or especially colourful, or those that had imposing statues of the Buddha. After seeing a few, their distinctiveness began to fade.

When Ashoka visited the place, a Buddhist monk, Upagupta, the son of a Varanasi perfumer, accompanied him. A story goes that Ashoka wanted to build 84,000 stupas on the same day and at the same hour. The Thera Yasas (elder monk), knowing these plans, hid the sun with his hand, allowing the construction to finish. This eclipse is important evidence in Ashokan chronology. At the sacred garden in Lumbini, he erected a pillar surmounted by the figure of a horse and exempted the village from virtually all taxes. On the pillar, he inscribed that he had come to offer reverence to Buddha's birthplace.

This later tour continued into Nepal as far as Kathmandu (Patan) and west to Shravasti, where Ashoka paid reverence to places where Buddha dwelt and preached. In Patan, he built a temple near the south side of the palace, and at each of the four sides of the city, he built four great hemispherical stupas. All seem to still be standing, although they may not be the originals. The seventy-foot-tall pillars Ashoka is thought to have erected there remain to be found. His daughter Charumati accompanied him; she married a Nepali and remained there as a nun, residing in a convent she built at Pashupatinath, a mile or two north of Kathmandu. A Charumati foundation attached to a stupa still exists.

Pillar at Lumbini *(Photo courtesy: Ashok Khanna)*

Rummindei Pillar, Commemoration of Visit to Buddha's Birthplace: *Twenty years after his coronation, Beloved-of-the-Gods, King Piyadasi, visited this place and worshipped because here the Buddha, the sage of the Sakyas, was born. He had a stone figure and a pillar set up and because the Lord was born here, the village of Lumbini was exempted from tax and required to pay only one eighth of the produce.*

Ashoka also visited Sarnath, where the Buddha preached his first sermon. It is a hamlet about six miles from the religious city of Varanasi, on the banks of the Ganges River. Ashoka is thought to have built stupas and monasteries there, and meditated in the main shrine. What remains of one of his pillars still stands near the shrine; its capital is displayed in the adjacent museum. That magnificent capital, with its four back-to-back lions, is the one that became the state emblem of India, immortalised in the national seal. Under the four lions is a wheel symbolising Buddhism, still featured in the centre of the Indian flag.

In its heyday, Sarnath had 1,500 monks and a stupa that stood 328 feet high. Centuries after Ashoka, redoubtable Chinese Buddhist monks made their own visits. On the afternoon of my arrival, a mere handful of people were sitting and chatting in the landscaped garden that surrounds the monuments. I was able to wander at leisure, imagining how it felt to be there in ancient times. The museum has several remarkable pieces from the Mauryan—and later Gupta—periods, but the stunning lion capital dominates the exhibit. Xuanzang, who visited in the seventh century CE, mentions a number of other monuments erected by Ashoka.

Although he was personally a follower of Buddha's teachings, Ashoka never forgot that his subjects included people of many races and religions, including Hellenes and Persians. He met with holy men of all sects on his tours, including Brahmans, whose elaborate rituals and ceremonies he did not favour. Ashoka's own views on tolerance, written in Edicts VII and XII, supported his wide-ranging discussions and consultations. This approach also allowed him to keep in touch with a broad cross-section of his population and a watchful eye on local officials.

Lion capital at Sarnath
(Photo courtesy: Adobe Stock)

Dhamma

Ashoka's first sets of edicts, inscribed on rocks, were issued about three to five years after the Kalinga War. They were unique and remarkable in his era—he was the first to speak directly in this way to people in his realm. Persian monarchs had communicated to the public with inscriptions, but only to celebrate their military conquests. Ashoka chose to spread his Dhamma, instead—the code of secular social ethics he developed after the war.

In synthesis, Dhamma emerges as a way of life based on humane social behaviour. Its bedrock was reverence for all forms of and approaches to life. It prescribed social behaviour that would allow all to live peacefully, in a tolerant society. Ashoka enjoined his subjects to abstain from killing, speak the truth, respect family and social relationships, especially toward the disadvantaged, tolerate other ways of life and live frugally. He mentions heaven and the next life possibly to help his subjects relate it to their own beliefs. Dhamma is non-theist and does not promote a fixed identity sort of soul as the agent of karma, ethical action or causation.

The Second Minor Rock Edict is a good summary of Dhamma: *'The king says that father and mother must be obeyed, respect for living creatures must be enforced, truth must be spoken, the teacher reverenced by the pupil and proper courtesy shown to relatives. These virtues of the law of piety must be observed.'*[18]

Biographers have commented extensively on Dhamma's origins. Some believe that it is the original teachings of the Buddha, prior to the theological superstructure that developed after his death. Ashoka, though, did not mention the Buddha in any edict propagating Dhamma, despite incorporating a Buddhist aura of kindness, compassion and charity. This may have been another effort at inclusivity—a way to keep his ideas broad enough to avoid offending the codes of any one cultural group, and his language understandable for his diverse population.[19]

Ashoka used Dhamma to consolidate and unify a far-flung empire. It was a set of civil ethics with a broader social intent: developing a moral citizenry without contradicting any organised religion, except in two critical areas. First, he believed in treating all people equally, regardless of caste, gender, class or nationality; and second, he exhorted against animal sacrifice.

Notably, he asked the state bureaucracy to spread the word, rather than Buddhist monks. This may, again, have been a way to avoid resentment among Brahmans and their followers, who were the most numerous among his subjects. Professor Olivelle believes that Ashoka was propagating a civil religion: What Buddha did for his followers, Ashoka tried to do for all people, regardless of their religious affiliations.[20]

It seems unlikely, though, that Ashoka's vigorous pursuit of Dhamma was merely strategic. It would be highly unusual for an intellectual agenda to sustain such consistent effort for so long. More likely, Ashoka's emotional insight after the Kalinga War affected how he looked at the world. Blessed with this insight (the gift of eye, as he put it) and following Buddha's example, he decided with genuine fervency to present his own life history as a model for the populace.[21]

Evidently, he had the same message sent out to various places in his realm, since inscriptions with precisely the same declarations have been discovered in locations distant from one another. In each capital, there were designated spokespeople who read Ashoka's messages to an assembly of citizens; expert artisans would then have inscribed the communications on prominent rocks or polished and sculpted pillars, erected in special places. The extraordinary height of the pillars, which required remarkable artistic and engineering skill, meant that they would be seen at some distance, and would be known to communicate important messages. Though many of the pillars were later toppled, and some were seriously damaged, the height of an intact one can be seen in the following image.

Ashoka Pillar at Lauriya Nandangarh
(Image courtesy: Deepika Rajjak)

Sanjeev Sanyal has recently expressed regret that the famous remorse edict, written after the war against the Kalingas, was not posted in that region, but only in others far away from the site of the battle. It's possible that the viceroy in that region decided not to post the declaration in order not to humiliate the territory's conquered population. Ashoka may well have made the same judgment. But, of course, many inscriptions may have simply been destroyed, or not yet found.

What seems clear is that, instead of trying to become a *balachakravartin* raja (a 'wheel-turning ruler') by conquering territory, like his father and grandfather, he chose to become an ideal Buddhist ruler—a Dhammaraja—and to conquer by spreading Dhamma. He wanted to rule without the use of force, and to promote compassion, justice and tolerance. He even dispatched Dhamma missions to Hellenic kings and border territories. In Edict XIII, he mentioned Antiochos II Theos of Syria, Ptolemy II Philadelphus of Egypt, Antigonus Gonatas of Macedonia, Magus of Cyrene and Alexander of Epirus. Other missions were sent to the Cholas, Cheras, Pandyas, Yonas, Kambojas, Nabhakas, Nabhitis, Bhojas, Pitinikas, Andhras and Palidas.

Ashoka issued no edicts that we know of in the last ten years of his life; his last seven pillar edicts were erected in his twenty-sixth and twenty-seventh regnal years. Although these edicts were still concerned with Dhamma, they were retrospective and introspective. He argued that people notice only their good deeds and not their misdeeds. But misdeeds do occur, and they should be noted and reckoned. Overall, he felt that it is good to maintain a positive balance, with many good deeds and few negligent ones. Importantly, even these late edicts show his awareness that promulgating regulations is not enough—he knew that persuasion, a long and difficult process, was essential to win his subjects' hearts and minds.

Monuments and Art

Art during Ashoka's reign attained a high standard. Lapidaries and goldsmiths were especially skilled; architects were capable of designing and erecting spacious and lofty edifices in brick, wood and stone. They could handle monoliths, construct embankments and sluice gates, and excavate commodious chambers. Gigantic shafts of sandstone were polished like jewels and joints of masonry precisely fitted. Notable buildings were richly adorned with decorative patterns and a variety of bas-reliefs; they held numerous statues of men and animals.

Ashoka's main architectural structures were probably built during the twelve years between the Rock and Pillar edicts. So imposing were these structures that a supernatural agency was thought by later visitors to have erected them. Faxian, in the early fifth century, reported: 'The royal palace and halls in the midst of the city, which exist now as of old, were all made by spirits which he employed, and which piled up the stones, reared the walls and gates, and executed the elegant carving and inlaid sculpture work, in a way no human hands of this world could accomplish.' Two hundred years later, Xuanzang, who visited it after the White Huns had ravaged the city, observed: 'The cloud-capped towers, the gorgeous palaces, the solemn temples…'[22]

Ashoka had a special fondness for monolithic pillars, with and without inscriptions. Many survive. Uniformity of style suggests craftsmen from the same region carved them. The pillars also reflect the king's personality and the ethos of his age. They range from thirty to forty feet high and are made of hard grey sandstone, chiselled and given a lustrous polish. Two such pillars grace the entrance to Sanchi. Animal capitals— lions, bulls, elephants, horses, geese—surmount their smooth, tapered shafts. These animals have symbolic meaning in Pali and Buddhist literature.

The custom of erecting pillars predated Ashoka, but he perfected the art. The Ashokan approach was revolutionary; for the first time, stone replaced wood for monumental sculpture. The Mauryas melded craftsmanship from the Achaemenid, Egyptian and Hellenic traditions with local methods. Ashoka's monoliths were frequently placed hundreds of miles away from quarries. Their exquisite finish bears testimony to the skill of the architects, stonecutters and transporters.[23] The aesthetic effect of Mauryan columns has never been surpassed in later Indian sculpture.

The best preserved among them is in Lauriya Nandangarh, in Bihar State. A seated lion, projecting an air of grandeur, tops it. The finest and most famous of the capitals is at Sarnath, with its four seated lions back-to-back on a round abacus that displays four animals—elephant, horse, bull and lion—and wheels between each carved relief. The lion, as king of the wild animals, was a symbol of royal sovereignty, and thus, the four back-to-back lions on the great pillar likely proclaimed Ashoka's rule in all directions. But the lion is also closely associated with the Buddha, so they could have signalled the spread of his message, as well. The scholar Balakrishna G. Gokhale has argued persuasively that Ashoka brilliantly used symbols like this to send both traditional Indian and Buddhist messages at once, thereby communicating to non-Buddhists in one way and to Buddhists in another. The bull was a symbol of strength, the elephant a symbol of patience and tranquillity, but they had additional special meanings for Buddhists.[24]

Pillar at Vaishali *(Photo courtesy: Ashok Khanna)*

Legend has it that Ashoka built 84,000 stupas. Xuanzang mentions a stupa in Afghanistan that rises to 300 feet, and one in Sri Lanka that exceeds 400 feet. They were surrounded by statuary and bas-reliefs that tell vivid stories. J.P. Vogel, in his book *Buddhist Art in India,* says: 'The history of Buddhist art does not really commence until the reign of the great Asoka, circa 250 BCE, two centuries and a quarter after Buddha's nirvana.'[25] Although he may not have built as many stupas and monasteries as the legends suggest, there is surely some truth to the tales— the second distribution of Buddha's relics occurred during his reign. His architecture also inspired stupas in Anuradhapura (Sri Lanka), Borobudur (Indonesia) and Bayon (Cambodia), among many others. The throne in the inner temple at Bodh Gaya and a small rail at Sarnath are also attributed to Ashoka, but not much is left to see.

Bayon Temple in Siem Reap, Cambodia *(Photo courtesy: Ashok Khanna)*

Seven cave dwellings belonging to Ashoka's era have been excavated with precision and deftness. Among them, those in the Barabar Hills near Bodh Gaya are the finest. These caves are truly artists' achievements, with carved semi-circular entrances, barrel-vaulted interiors and walls polished to a glassy smoothness. They served as a refuge for monks during the rains. The idea for them may have come from Egypt, via Persia.

Last Years

In his twenty-ninth regnal year, Ashoka's chief queen, Asandhimitta, died. Four years later, Tissarakha was elevated to chief queen. She was an unprincipled young woman, according to legend; she cast amorous glances at her stepson Kunala, who was renowned for the beauty of his eyes. Finding him alone, she declared: 'I get a burning feeling inside, as though a forest fire were consuming a dry wood.'[26] Kunala, though, repulsed the queen's incestuous advances, and she became afraid that if he succeeded Ashoka, he would punish her. Soon thereafter, the king deputed Kunala to Taxila, and then found himself overcome by a dangerous disease. Tissarakha set out to find a cure and ultimately succeeded in saving Ashoka's life. During his illness, for a short period, the queen was granted sovereign powers.

Using the king's seal, she wrote to the viceroy's ministers in Taxila, directing them to put out Kunala's eyes and exile him and his wife to the mountains. On seeing the king's seal, Kunala asked the confused ministers to carry out his father's order. Blinded, he left Taxila with his wife. In the course of their wanderings, they came to Pataliputra and managed to penetrate the inner court of the palace. There, Kunala wept and sang a sad song. The king, on hearing the song, sent for the singer and recognised his son.

Discovering what his wife had done, Ashoka wanted to 'tear out her eyes, rip open her body with sharp rakes, impale her alive on a spit, cut off her nose with a saw, cut out her tongue with a razor.'[27] Despite Kunala interceding on her behalf, Ashoka had her burned alive in a lacquer house and punished everyone else involved. Her behaviour had caused a severe injury to his son, deprived him of ever becoming king (as no blind person could be, according to the custom of the era) and reminded Ashoka of his ugliness, reigniting the wounds of rejection. His response, if legends are to be believed, was unrestrained—punishing her by burning her alive went against his fundamental beliefs and everything he had worked for.

Ashoka declared Kunala's son Samprati the heir apparent. As an act of atonement for executing Tissarakha, he made prodigious donations to the Buddhist Order. The crown prince, though, colluded with ministers to stop these donations, which threatened to deplete the treasury. Ashoka then began to give away other valuables, such as gold plates. When he ran out of precious metal, he summoned the ministers and asked them, 'Who is the king?' They said, he was the king. Ashoka burst into tears and said they were being kind, but it was not true. 'Today,' he said, 'I am no longer obeyed; no matter how many commands I think of issuing, they are all countermanded just like a river that is turned back when it dashes against a mountain cliff.'[28]

One day, a *bhikkhu* (mendicant) came around asking for alms. The only thing Ashoka could give him was half a myrobalan fruit. 'Behold,' he said, 'this is my last gift; to this pass have come the riches of the emperor of India. My royalty and power have departed; deprived of health, of physic and of physicians, to me no support is left save that of the assembly of saints. Eat this fruit, which is offered with the intent that the whole assembly may partake of it, my last gift.'

The social anthropologist S.J. Tambiah described the encounter in this poem:[29]

> The conqueror of the world entire,
> The giver of a hundred crores.
> The happy king had in the end,
> A half myrobalan as his realm.
> Bound by the body he, the sorrowless king,
> Sank into sorrow facing death, when as
> The sum of his good works came to an end.

Lahiri quotes a poem from the vantage of an elder member of the Sangha:[30]

> A great donor, the lord of men,
> the eminent Maurya, Asoka,
> has gone from being lord of Jumbudvipa
> to being lord of half a myrobalan,
> Today this lord of the earth,
> his sovereignty stolen by his servants
> presents the gift of just half a myrobalan,
> as though reproving the common folk
> whose hearts are puffed up
> with a passion for enjoying great splendour.

The story suggests that Ashoka died a sad, disappointed and depressed man, divested of his power. He was propelled to greatness by his first love, but undone by his last.

CHAPTER 6

The Decline and Fall of the Mauryan Empire

The Mauryan dynasty ended around 180 BCE with the assassination of Brihadratha, the sixth emperor to follow Ashoka, by Pushyamitra, his Brahman general, who founded the Shunga Empire. The names and terms of the rulers who led the empire for the fifty years between Ashoka's death and Brihadratha's assassination are mired in confusion. Bactrian Greeks had begun to threaten the Mauryans from the north and Andhras from the south. Quite possibly, several tribes west of the Indus River broke away to form independent principalities. There is no evidence that any of his successors followed Ashoka's policy of Dhamma and non-violence. Still, his grandson Dasharatha, his immediate successor, also supported the Ajivikas, and was the last ruler in India to do so. He had caves excavated for them to use as shelters in the rainy season in perpetuity, and declared his support with inscriptions on the walls of the polished chambers. However, soon after his reign, the dedications were erased or marred, presumably by followers of other religions.

Why did the Mauryan Empire disintegrate so quickly after Ashoka's death? R. Thapar has an elaborate discussion of this issue in her book *Asoka and the Decline of the Mauryas*.[1] In summary, many historians blame his high-minded policies for the empire's rapid decline. They believe Ashoka's dedication to non-violence, Buddhism and Dhamma made the empire vulnerable to revolt from within and attack from without. Governance became too effete to hold together such a vast territory. Other commentators believe that the economy started to decline after Ashoka's time, until the empire became untenable. It's also possible that the Brahman community, a very powerful group, may have ultimately been behind the fall. Ashoka had undercut their social standing by following Buddha's teaching, preaching Dhamma and appointing Dhamma *Mahamattas* with substantial social authority. He had also eroded their income by banning animal sacrifice and discouraging their ceremonies, rituals and festivals. And, of course, his family was of lower-caste origin and, therefore, always suspect. It was this seething resentment that may have finally erupted when the Brahman Pushyamitra assassinated Brihadratha, the last Mauryan ruler.

Are these reasons for the empire's demise plausible? While Ashoka was dedicated to non-violence, he seems to have kept his vast army intact. As none of his successors followed his philosophy, there was no barrier to using that large force to put down revolts or invasions. If his policies were at fault, the collapse should have happened sooner. Ashoka was also careful to pay consistent respect to Brahmans. If they had wanted to revolt, it is hard to see why they would have waited fifty years after his death. As a relatively compact, organised and literate community, they could have acted immediately, especially during the confusion caused by the initial succession. Finally, the evidence suggests that Mauryan taxes were not excessive and that the kingdom's economy prospered during Ashoka's reign and after his death.

Perhaps the most obvious initial cause for the empire's decline was the partition and subsequent reunification. It must have disrupted management of the administration, the economy and the army. The Mauryan realm was already an artificial entity, created by conquest of an ethnically and culturally diverse people at different levels of development. No concept of national identity existed. Groups gave allegiance to rulers if they benefited and they broke away if they did not. Thus, the empire's management was critical for its continued existence. Rulers had to protect groups from each other and from outsiders, and facilitate economic growth by expanding markets. Administration was fairly centralised in metropolitan areas, but less so in the core and peripheral areas. This structure thrived under Ashoka who seems to have been a great politician and administrator who also attracted the loyalty of his subjects because of his concern for their welfare. Being the third in a line of good administrators is a great record for any dynasty. Mauryan luck ran out after him. At the end of Ashoka's reign, it became difficult to administer the huge empire. His successors may not have been as capable as the first three Mauryas and they did not rule for long enough to improve or win their subjects' loyalty. The empire could well have declined because of inadequate management.

CHAPTER 7
Ashoka's Legacy

Buddhism, Non-violence, Tolerance and Governance

Ashoka's greatest achievement remains underrated: he preached and practiced Dhamma while successfully steering a vast empire that enjoyed peace and prosperity for almost three decades. It was a bold experiment and a unique adventure in governance, unparalleled in known human history. Ambition may have led him to acquiesce to a coup and violence to consolidate his position, and anger at his wife's betrayal toward the end of his life may have driven him to order her execution for a heinous crime, but he was not the wantonly cruel king some have claimed him to be. Such speculation should not tarnish the clear vision and character that Ashoka displays in his remarkable personal edicts.

Ashoka's deep reverence for life filtered down to concern for all human beings and animals. It infused his entire administration. Despite his own emotional commitment to Buddhism, he actively promoted all religions followed by his culturally varied subjects, and encouraged their peaceful coexistence. He sought to ensure equal justice for all by eliminating judicial and caste biases. He reformed rules for prisoners condemned to death and released others on the anniversary of his coronation. To facilitate harmony, Ashoka provided ethical norms for behaviour within families, with friends and teachers, and toward servants. He took care of the disadvantaged, appointed special ministers for women and prohibited killing animals. All this was achieved with introspection. Consistently doing good is as difficult as recognising one's shortcomings. Nevertheless, he persevered, recognising that regulation would not be as successful as persuasion. He also left another enormous legacy, which has endured for 2,300 years: Ashoka's sponsorship of Buddhism propelled its development of an international following.

Rulers have used his commitment to non-violence as an example, but sparingly, too sparingly. Still, his even-handed treatment of all religions and people is now codified in the constitutions of many countries, including the country of his birth. Bruce Rich, in his book *To Uphold the World,* argues that Ashoka was a forerunner of a number of modern concepts of human rights, including due process, equal protection under the law and religious tolerance. He also anticipated modern environmental concerns, such as the protection of animals and forests. Rich quotes Albert Schweitzer's description of ethics and reverence for life: 'A man is ethical only when life, as such, is sacred to him, that of plants and animals as well as that of fellow man.' Ashoka's inscriptions echo these sentiments.

As John Strong has observed: 'Ashoka's deeds altered his worldview, and gave him an insight into his essence: His greatness is in what he did and what he made possible, not what he claimed to be.'[1] He was more than two millennia ahead of his time.

Here are some excerpts from his edicts and inscriptions:[2]

Buddhism

Bhabra Inscription: *You know how deep is my respect for and faith in the Buddha, Dhamma and the Sangha. Whatever was spoken by Lord Buddha, was well-spoken. I desire that the sermons on Dhamma be heard by many monks and nuns and laymen and laywomen. I am having this engraved so that you may know what I desire.*

Schism Edict: *The Beloved-of-the-Gods, orders the officers of Kausambi/Pataliputra thus: No one is to cause dissension in the Order. The Order of monks and nuns has been united, and this unity should last for as long as my sons and great grandsons and the moon and the sun....*

Non-violence

Thirteenth Major Rock Edict: *When he had been consecrated eight years, Devanampiya Piyadasi conquered Kalinga. Many were killed and deported. After that, he earnestly practiced Dhamma and felt remorse about Kalinga. All the suffering, violence, murder, and separation from loved ones—even those that escaped suffered the misfortunes of their friends and relatives. Devanampiya believes that one who has done wrong should be forgiven, as far as it is possible to forgive. Devanampiya wishes that all beings should be unharmed, self-controlled, calm in mind and gentle.*

Eleventh Major Rock Edict: *There is no gift comparable to the gift of Dhamma, praising it, sharing it, and fellowship in it. And this is good behaviour, generosity toward all and abstention from killing. By so doing, there is gain in this world, and in the next, there is infinite merit, through the gift of Dhamma.*

First Major Rock Edict: *Against killing, sacrifice and festivals. The king's kitchen used much meat before Dhamma, but now only two peacocks and a deer are used, and this killing will cease in the future.*

Tolerance

Twelfth Major Rock Edict: *The king honours all sects. Each sect should honour the others as it increases the influence of one's own and benefits that of the other. Therefore, concord is to be commended, so that men may hear one another's principles and obey them. All sects should be well informed, and should teach that which is good, and that everywhere their adherents should be told: 'The king does not consider gifts or honour to be as important as the progress of the essential doctrines of all sects.'*

Seventh Major Rock Edict: *Devanampiya Piyadasi wishes that all sects may dwell in all places, for all seek self-control and purity of the mind....*

Governance

Sixth Major Rock Edict: *At all times, whether I am eating, or in the women's apartments, or in my inner apartments, or at the cattle shed, or in my carriage, or in my gardens—wherever I may be, my informants should keep me in touch with public business. In hard work and dispatch of business alone, I find no satisfaction, however. For I must promote the welfare of the whole world, and hard work and dispatch of business are the means of doing so. And whatever may be my great deeds, I have done them in order to discharge my debt to all beings.*

First Separate Edict: *To the officers and city magistrates at Tosali/ Sampa. You are in charge of many thousands of living beings. You* *should gain the affections of men. Often a man suffers imprisonment or torture without reason and then he is released from prison. He suffers and many other people suffer. You should strive to practice impartiality, be even-tempered and not rash. He who is slack will not act, and in your official functions, you must strive, act and work. Thus, you must see to it that men are never imprisoned or tortured without good reason. For this purpose, I will send officers on tour every five years to see these instructions are carried out. The princes at Ujjain and Taxila will send officers every three years.*

Seventh Pillar Edict: *...On the roads, I have had banyan trees planted, which will give shade to beasts and men. I have had mango groves planted and wells dug and rest houses built at every eight kilometres. I have had many watering places made for the use of man and beast. I have done these things in order that my people might conform to Dhamma.*

My officers of Dhamma are busy in many matters of public benefit and among members of all sects. These and other officers are busy with the distribution of charity on behalf of the queen, my sons, princes and myself. Thus, the glory of Dhamma will increase throughout the world, and it will be endorsed in the form of mercy, charity, truthfulness, purity, gentleness and virtue.

The advancement of Dhamma amongst men has been achieved by legislation and persuasion. Of the two, legislation has been less effective and persuasion more so....

Art

B.G. Gokhale, in his biography of Ashoka, says Ashokan art is 'a flower of a rare personal initiative and exotic nourishment.'[3] His edicts are the best remaining examples of Mauryan art. The pillar at Lauriya Nandangarh, a shaft of polished sandstone topped with a seated lion, is the best preserved and projects grandeur.

Another capital found in an early excavation of Pataliputra shows Hellenic and Achaemenid (Persian) influences. But the finest is the lion capital at Sarnath, with its four back-to-back lions on a circular abacus that has four other animals and wheels carved in relief below.

Originally, the lions supported a large stone wheel above them (as in the emblem of the Supreme Court of India), symbolising Buddha's wheel of law. It also symbolised Ashoka's aspiration to be a chakravartin (a 'wheel-turning ruler', a Buddhist ideal) propagating Dhamma. The *Asokavadana* and other sources portray Ashoka as an iron-wheeled chakravartin, one who rules one continent of the real, imperfect world (as opposed to the mythical golden-wheeled chakravartin who rules over the whole world as a utopia, the silver-wheeled chakravartin who rules over three of the world's four continents, and the copper-wheeled chakravartin who promoted *Dhamma* in the *Sangha* and in the spiritual and personal realms). John Strong and other scholars agree that chakravartins were all dhammarajas, ruling justly and impartially, with Dhamma as their mandate. To be a chakravartin is the secular equivalent of being a Buddha.

The earliest available examples of Indian architecture are from Ashoka's reign. He commissioned cave dwellings carved from solid rock. A series of chambers near Bodh Gaya were carved to duplicate wood construction as dwellings for ascetics; the most noteworthy are the Lomas Rishi and Sudama caves. While Mauryan gloss sculpture disappeared soon after Ashoka, the cave architecture remained for a millennium. (*Indian Art* by R.C. Craven is the best source on this.)

Ashoka's life and work have also inspired modern Indian artists. The Chaitya Art Gallery in the ITC Maurya in New Delhi displays an imposing statue of Ashoka at Kalinga by Meera Mukherjee, showing his remorse at the moment of victory:

Ashoka at Kalinga by Meera Mukherjee
(Photo courtesy: Amitabha Bhattacharya, Courtesy of Maurya Sheraton)

Ramachandran's bronze and zinc statue of Ashoka, based on his inscriptions, also shows the king's remorse after the war. And M.F. Hussain's tapestry brings to life Ashoka's struggle between war and peace.

Ashoka's Struggle by M.F. Hussain
(Photo courtesy: Amitabha Bhattacharya, Courtesy of Maurya Sheraton)

Legacy in Asia

Buddhist Kingship

Buddha grew up in a republic, and he respected its collective approach to governance. But powerful monarchical states emerged during his life, and began to dominate the republics. While he favoured the republican form of government, Buddha gave importance to the role of a righteous monarch, as well. For him, a king was a mortal man who derived his authority from the people to rule in their name for their good, an early version of a social contract concept of kingship.

The Jataka stories, Buddhist tales of the Buddha's previous lives, describe an ideal king as one who rules with selflessness, rectitude, mercy and equal respect for all beings. He is responsible for the moral fabric of society, which he upholds through his personal righteousness, and for the economic welfare of the people, through which he ensures full employment. In short, he applies Buddhist ethics to state administration in order to effect Dhamma, allowing for an unqualified supremacy of the moral law over government affairs (Dhammaraj). This is in sharp contrast to the Brahman approach, which saw kings as semi-divine and working on their personal salvation by doing their proper duty to their subjects (Rajadharma).[4]

Bimbisara, king of the powerful kingdom of Magadha, and a contemporary of the Buddha, was partial to his teaching. His son, Ajatashatru, a parricide, was also a contemporary and, in tradition, thought to have reformed later in his life. The first two Buddhist Councils, at Rajagriha soon after Buddha's passing, and at Vaishali a century later, were both held in Magadha. Although there is no mention of either of these kings ruling in accordance with Dhamma, much of the conceptual development of Buddhist righteous kingship is thought to have sprung from observation of their kingdoms, before Ashoka's time. He made it a reality, restructuring social consciousness and behaviour to conform to Buddhist notions of equality, compassion and dignity for all living beings, and building a Buddhist civilisation that was devoted to improving the welfare of its citizens. Dhamma is central to Ashoka's edicts, and their spirit of active social concern, religious tolerance, ecological awareness, common ethical concepts and renunciation of war.[5]

Legend has it that Ashoka's son Mahinda, who had been ordained as a Buddhist monk, was sent by Moggaliputta, the head of the Third Buddhist Council, to modern Sri Lanka, where he successfully expounded the Buddha's teachings to the king, Devanampiya Tissa, who accepted them. Later, Mahinda's sister Sanghamitta brought a branch of the Bodhi Tree to Sri Lanka and preached to the royal ladies, converting them to the faith as well. By the end of Mahinda's life, about forty-eight years after his arrival, Sri Lanka had become a Buddhist state-civilisation patterned after Ashoka's. A chronicle shows that the three Sri Lankan kings in the first half of the first century BCE continued being agents of Dhamma.[6] Arguably, the pattern has persisted on and off through much of the succeeding centuries, with interruptions of foreign rule, up to modern times.

The Shunga dynasty, which succeeded the Mauryan, was itself eventually displaced by the southward expansion of Greco-Bactrian kingdoms, culminating in the rule of Menander I, whose territory stretched from Gandhara into the north west part of the Indian subcontinent. His capital was at Sagala—modern Sialkot, in Pakistan. Dates are fuzzy, but he ruled for about twelve years between 165 BCE and 130 BCE. He was considered a benevolent ruler and may have become a Buddhist, although that is controversial—stories told of Buddha and Ashoka are in other sources ascribed to Menander instead.

Buddhist tradition as described in the Pali text, *Milinda Panha*, or 'Questions of Menander', states that he accepted Buddhism after discussions with Nagasena, a monk, and abdicated the throne to become a monk himself. (Historian W.W. Tarn does not accept this version, though Plutarch preserves the story of Menander's benevolent rule).[7] That he was a follower is bolstered by the use of Buddhist symbols in his coinage and his acceptance of the title Dhammaraja, also used by Ashoka. And, of course, in Menander's time, Ashoka's inscriptions, written in Brahmi, Greek and Kharoshti, could still be read. Stimulated by Menander's patronage and that of his successors, Buddhist ideas and representations may have begun to spread to Central Asia, accompanied by Ashoka's legend of righteous rule.

The Kushan dynasty started in the first century CE in Central Asia, and gradually expanded to modern Afghanistan, Pakistan and North Central India, possibly all the way to Pataliputra, the Mauryan capital. For a period, Kushan territory also included Kashgar, Khotan and Yarkand, Chinese dependencies in the Tarim Basin in modern Xinjiang, China. Kanishka (127–140 CE), its renowned ruler, embraced the diverse cultural influences of his empire, including Greco-Bactrian cults and Zoroastrianism, but he was partial to Buddhism and close to Ashvaghosha, a scholar. Stories similar to those told of Ashoka are attributed to him as well, such as the prophecy of his birth, the change in behaviour after his conversion to Buddhism, and his role presiding over the Fourth Buddhist Council held in Kashmir. Ashoka's edicts were apparently still readable during this period—the Kushans used Brahmi and Prakrit, the script and language used by Ashoka, for their administration. Kanishka encouraged Greco-Buddhist art and his coinage depicted Buddha in the Greco-Buddhist style. He was highly respected by his subjects because of his kindness, humility and sense of equality. His stupa in Peshawar, Pakistan, is considered a seminal contribution to Buddhist architecture.

Spread of Buddhism

Gandhara, in modern Afghanistan, was in a sense the birthplace of Buddhism as a world religion. The Kushans controlled the silk roads into Western China and the transmission of Buddhism to the East is generally thought to have begun during their period. As Buddhist merchants settled in China, their beliefs aroused the curiosity of locals. Later, the merchants brought in monks as advisors and teachers, and the local populations gradually adopted the philosophy. Over time, monasteries developed, giving merchants a place to rest on their journeys, and the locals' education and medical treatment. Powerful monarchs adopted Buddhism, and patronage persuaded their subjects to follow suit. Importantly, the religion spread peacefully, with a message of compassion, while adapting to the cultural dispositions of different peoples.

The two main historical strands of Buddhism are Hinayana, which emphasises personal salvation or achieving nirvana as the goal, and Mahayana, which stresses working to become a Bodhisattva (Buddha to be), and foregoing full enlightenment until all humankind is ready for salvation. The Hinayana Tradition spread from India to Central Asia and China and later fused with Mahayana, which became the dominant form of Buddhism and itself spread to Korea, Japan and Vietnam, and along sea trade routes to Malaysia, Indonesia, Cambodia and South China. A separate Tibetan Mahayana Tradition started in the seventh century, and spread through the Himalayan regions to Bhutan, parts of Central Asia, Mongolia and some regions of Russia. Finally, Mahayana also spread from the second century CE along the sea trade routes from India to Vietnam, Malaysia, Indonesia, Cambodia and South China. Thus, Mahayana developed in regions of India where Buddhism was exposed to non-Indian influences; the cross-fertilisation made it more acceptable in other cultures. A strand of Hinayana Buddhism known as the Theravada Tradition spread to Sri Lanka during Ashoka's time, and perhaps also to Myanmar and Thailand, and centuries later became the main Buddhist tradition in South East Asia. The notion of Buddhist kingship travelled along with the philosophy/religion, as well, although the idea of Dhammaraj was adopted more fully by the Theravada Tradition, which emphasised values to be expressed in the social, political and economic life of society.

China, Korea, Japan and Vietnam

Among the legends about Buddhism's arrival in China is a story in *Fayuan Zhulin,* a Buddhist encyclopaedia (668 CE), about Ashoka sending a deputation of monks led by the teacher Shilifang to present a number of sutras to the first emperor of the Qin dynasty (221–206 BCE). Ashoka probably was not aware of China at all, nor even still alive by that time. Emperor Ming, in 65 CE, echoed one of Ashoka's edicts with a decree that anyone suspected of a capital crime should be given a chance for redemption, but a connection between them is unlikely. Kushan missionaries such as Lokaksema, though, are known to have travelled to the Chinese capital Luoyang (and perhaps also to Nanjing) around 178 CE, and Parthian merchant An Xuan and monk An Shigao also came at around the same time, and translated Buddhist sutras.

China was a sophisticated culture; the absorption of Buddhism was gradual but momentous. Elite monks applied Buddhist ideas to issues raised by Confucian and Taoist followers, fusing Buddhism with those philosophies and adding a civil society dimension to their emphasis on family and governance. Scholars and monks were sufficiently interested to travel all the way to India, an extremely arduous journey, to bring back literature for translation.

The first Chinese monk to be ordained was Zhu Zixing, in about 260 CE, and the first Chinese pilgrims were Yu Falan and Yu Daosui, who set out a decade apart, starting in 325 CE, trying to reach India by sea. They died in Indo-China. Kumarajiva (344–413 CE), partly of Indian origin, was taken by a conquering Chinese general to the capital, Chang'an, where he directed a translation bureau. Perhaps the most famous monk was Bodhidharma (440–528 CE), who founded the Chan sect of Buddhism and, in legend, the Shaolin monks and Kung Fu.

Most important for Indian history were the journeys of Faxian and Xuanzang. Faxian set out in 399 CE, visiting India, Sri Lanka and Java, and returned to China by sea in 413 CE. He wrote an account of his travels, *Foguoji* (*Record of Buddhist Countries*). Xuanzang (602–664 CE) came to India along the Northern Silk Road, and went back about sixteen years later along the Southern one. His account, *Xiyuji* (*Record of Western Regions*), was the basis of a sixteenth-century novel, *Xiyouji* (*Journey to the West*). Back in Chang'an, he devoted his life to translating the works he had collected. Information from his travelogue was used by the British to discover several Buddhist sites in India.[8]

By the fifth century CE, Ashoka's approach to governance had been widely adopted by Central Asian and Northern Chinese rulers, most strikingly by the Southern Chinese Emperor Wu of Liang (502–549 CE), whose rule shows many elements of influence. A statue of Ashoka from that period has been found in Chengdu, with an identifying inscription. Ashoka's appeal as a model ruler continued through the Sui and Tang dynasties. Emperor Wen-ti of Sui (581–604 CE) was devoted to the political and religious ideal embodied by Ashoka; he was a Buddhist who also followed Confucianism. Wen's son, Yang, continued his tradition of Buddhist righteous rule.

Emperor Taizong (629–649 CE) of the Tang dynasty, which followed the Sui dynasty, supported Buddhism by building several monasteries. It was during his reign that Xuanzang travelled to India. The dynasty was interrupted by the rule of Empress Wu Zetian (690–705 CE), who took Ashoka as her model ruler.[9]

In ancient Korea, Buddhism received royal recognition in Paekche in the fourth century and in Silla in the fifth century. Silla King Jinhueng (540–576 CE), in his later years, became a Buddhist monk. In the seventh century, when Korea unified under the Silla dynasty, elements of Buddhism, Confucianism, Taoism and local shaman practices were fused into a common ideology. It was under the Koryo dynasty (tenth to fourteenth centuries CE) that Buddhism gained prominence. The founding king, Wang Kon (918–943 CE), regarded the Buddhist Dharma as the basis for his reign, and began an exam for monks to prepare them for advising the court. In 1036 CE, an edict abolished the death penalty and decreed that one out of four sons had to become a monk. From the fourteenth century to the early twentieth century, the Yi/Choson dynasty gave precedence to neo-Confucianism as the state ideology; Christian influence started to grow in the nineteenth century. With Korea's economic success, Buddhism has been resurgent.

Vietnam had its own links to Buddhism and India from the first century CE. One of the earliest Buddhist missionaries to China was from the Indian community in Chiao-chih, in North Vietnam, where texts from India were translated in a monastery that also offered training for monks. Chinese monks unable to travel to India would often come to Chiao-chih. Buddhism functioned as Vietnam's national religion from the tenth to the fourteenth centuries CE. One ruler of the Ly dynasty, a one-time temple orphan, appointed monks to his governing council. After the Le dynasty (1428–1788 CE) was established, Confucianism became the official ideology, but the vast majority of the population remained Buddhist. Although many Vietnamese became Catholics during the French occupation of Indo-China from the mid-nineteenth to the mid-twentieth centuries, about eighty per cent of the population remains Buddhist today.

The first record of Buddhism reaching Japan is from 552 CE, when a Paekche king from Korea sent Buddhist sutras and statues to the imperial court. Not long afterward, Prince Shotuku (573–621 CE), regarded as the founder of Japanese Buddhism, shepherded its adoption as the state religion. As advisor to Empress Suiko, he issued a document about governance, fusing Buddhist and Confucian ideas, that came to be known as his constitution. Many of its clauses resemble Ashoka's edicts, and Shotuku's other policies also resemble the Buddhist civilisation that Ashoka tried to create. Over time, Buddhism, Confucianism and Shinto ideas and practices fused. During the Meiji period (1868–1945 CE), Shinto ideas dominated, but after World War II, the Shinto state was dissolved, and Japan adopted Zen (Cha'an) Buddhist concentration and Confucian devotion to social duty to propel its economic success. Gradually, it became a secular society, although ninety per cent funeral rites are conducted by Buddhist monks, giving rise to the term 'Funeral Buddhism'.

Tibet, Mongolia and Bhutan

The first Tibetan monarch credited with introducing Buddhism was Songtsen Gam-po, in the seventh century. He made Tibet the dominant power in Central Asia through control of the Silk Road. Tibetan armies captured Chang'an and the translation centre along the Silk Road in the late eighth century; the king at the time, Trisong Detsen (755–797 CE), sent emissaries to India, China and Central Asia to get Buddhist texts, invited scholars to his court and built monasteries. King Yeshe-Od (967–1040 CE) revived interest in the religion, eventually abdicating and becoming a monk.

Missionaries from Nepal and Central Asia brought Buddhism to Mongolia in the early centuries CE, but it became broadly accepted only when the emperors of the Yuan dynasty established in the thirteenth and fourteenth centuries converted to Tibetan Buddhism. Mongolian chronicles from that period cite Ashoka as a model for kingship. In 1587, Sonam Gyatso, head of a Tibetan school, converted the Mongol ruler Altan Khan and was given the title of Dalai Lama. As the religion spread, Mongols and others from the Central steppes regarded Lhasa as their cultural and religious capital. It was under the fifth Dalai Lama that Buddhist political power over Tibet was achieved and Dharma governance established. Although in exile from Tibet, the fourteenth and current Dalai Lama is the most visible and influential exponent of Buddhism worldwide. He has said that his most important commitments are to compassion, forgiveness, tolerance, contentment and self-discipline, and that: 'Tibetan culture is a culture of peace, a culture of non-violence.' His approach is consonant with Ashoka's in every respect.

India

Though its rulers were partial to Hinduism, Buddhism and Buddhist art flourished in India once again under the Gupta dynasty, which ruled the northern swath of the subcontinent from the fourth to the sixth centuries. After the Guptas, the region split into small kingdoms that were reunified in the early seventh century under Harshavardhana, who ruled from 606–647 CE. He is thought to have been either a Shaivite (a devotee of Shiva) or eclectic religiously, but according to Xuanzang, who visited his court, he became a Buddhist at some stage and, like Ashoka, banned animal slaughter, built rest houses for travellers and poor people and organised an annual assembly of scholars.

Nalanda, the Buddhist university where Xuanzang spent a couple of years, flourished during this period. At its peak, it attracted scholars from Central Asia, Korea, China and Tibet. Support for Buddhism then entered the doldrums until the rise of the Pala dynasty, which ruled the modern area of Bengal, Bihar, Bangladesh and Nepal from about the eighth to the eleventh century. They supported Nalanda and Vikramashila universities, and established several monasteries. Buddhist scholars travelled abroad to teach, such as Atisha to Tibet and Sumatra, and there was contact with the Sailendra dynasty of Java.

Around the turn of the first millennium, Turkic Muslims began raiding northwest India and extending their conquests to the south and east. Local monarchies were eliminated and Buddhist monasteries destroyed, both crucial supports for the religion. Moreover, after almost two millennia of coexistence, the lines between Buddhism and other Indian religions had blurred, each absorbing aspects of the others. The final blows came with Bhaktiyar Khilji's destruction and looting of Vikramashila and Nalanda universities and the fall of the Pala dynasty. Although the religion lingered in places for two or three centuries, it declined as a spiritual force in India. No longer able to look to India for guidance, other Buddhist countries began to separate doctrinally and institutionally.

South East Asia

Buddhism may have come to South East Asia during Ashoka's rule, when the Buddhist Council sent missions to Myanmar and Thailand. In any case, it certainly entered the region in the early centuries of the Common Era with traders from India and Sri Lanka, and later through contact with China. In the eighth and ninth centuries CE, Indianised states' empires were established that practiced Hinduism, Mahayana Buddhism and indigenous animist beliefs. Among them were: Champa (second to fifteenth centuries CE) in modern Vietnam and Cambodia; Funan (third to sixth centuries CE) in modern Vietnam, Cambodia and Thailand; Srivijaya (seventh to thirteenth centuries CE) in Indonesia (Sumatra) and Malaysia (Malacca); Sailendra (eighth to ninth centuries CE) in Indonesia (Java); and Khmer (ninth to fifteenth centuries CE) in Cambodia, Laos, Thailand and Vietnam. Sailendra kings were ardent patrons of Buddhism, erecting numerous monuments, including those in Borobudur. Yijing, a Chinese monk who travelled to Pelambang, the capital of the Sailendra Empire, in about 680 CE, testified to the importance of Buddhism in the kingdom.

Jayavarman VII (1181–1218 CE) of the Khmers built Bayon in Angkor, in modern-day Cambodia, which has bas-reliefs depicting citizens' daily lives and intended to show compassion, consistent with inscriptions showing concern for their suffering. Like Ashoka, he built hospitals, as well. Jayavarman conceived of himself as a Bodhisattva king. This concept had a long life in Cambodian and Thai politics.

The kingdom of Pagan, in modern Myanmar, came into prominence under King Aniruddha (1040–1077 CE), when he brought most of the country and the Nanchao area of South China under his control. Pagan developed in the shadow of the Nanchao dynasty, which subscribed to Buddhism; its kings claimed descent from Ashoka.[10] Aniruddha is credited with introducing the Pali Canon and Theravada Buddhism to his kingdom, partly by importing monks from Sri Lanka. In the thirteenth century CE, King Dhammaraja sent a mission to Bodh Gaya to revive the Mahabodhi Temple, which had fallen into disrepair. He alluded to Ashoka as the original builder. Five centuries later, in 1875, King Mindon (1853–1878 CE) sought permission from the local rulers to do so again, and also cited Ashoka. Like Ashoka, he claimed that he had illuminated the wheel of the conqueror.[11]

Buddhist rulers from Myanmar all the way to Japan also followed Ashoka as builders of stupas as symbols of righteous rule. Two major stupas are Shwedagon Paya in Yangon, Myanmar, and Pha That Luang in Vientiane, Laos. The legend of Shwedagon Paya, in Yangon, has it that two merchant brothers met the Buddha, who gave them eight hairs to bring back to Myanmar to be enshrined. With the help of the ruling king, these hairs were put in a golden casket and a golden stupa was built over it. In time, the stupa fell into disuse, but later, King Ashoka visited Myanmar and was able to find it with difficulty, as it was shrouded by a jungle. He had the jungle cleared and the stupa restored.[12]

Shwedagon Paya, Yangon *(Photo courtesy: Ashok Khanna)*

In Sri Lanka, King Parakarama II, who ascended to the throne in 1236 CE, recognising the decline of Buddhism in India, commissioned a venerable monk to revive the original teachings, which became the Theravada orthodoxy and influenced Sri Lanka and South East Asia through to the modern era. The doctrine included Ashoka's ideas of Dhammaraj governance. Theravada Buddhist kings were subject to Dhamma, and some used Dhammaraja or Ashoka in their titles.

Buddha, Pollonaruwa *(Photo courtesy: Ashok Khanna)*

King Ram Kamheng (1279–1298 CE) of the Sukhothai period in Thailand is thought to have replicated Ashokan traditions mentioned in the *Mahavamsa*, such as ordering that he could be disturbed anywhere, even in his toilet, for urgent business. Later, Ayutthaya rulers continued his traditions, affirming the role of kingship as the expression of Dhamma. King Tiloka (1441–1487 CE) of Lan Na (Chiang Mai, Thailand) supported Buddhism, and in 1447 CE temporarily renounced the throne to enter the monastic order.

Replica of Ashoka Pillar at Wat Umong, Chiang Mai, Thailand
(Photo courtesy: L. Roychoudhury)

All the kings of Lan Sang in Laos also sought to be dhammarajas. Setthathirat, in 1566 CE, built Pha That Luang temple in Vientiane to reinforce the Dhammaraj concept; it was said to be on the site of an ancient stone pillar erected by Ashoka that contained a relic of Buddha, supposedly brought by missionaries sent by Ashoka in the third century BCE.

Pha That Luang, Vientiane (*Photo courtesy: Adobe Stock*)

Post-Colonial

Historian M. Deeg says that: 'Rulers in Asia in different contexts and to different degrees could successfully apply and adopt elements from [Ashoka's] life in their own process of self-definition and self-legitimation without even mentioning the name of the Mauryan ruler, and it is this very aspect that might well be his hidden but most powerful legacy in Asian history in and beyond South Asia.'[13] Prime Minister U Nu, in Burma, and President Bandaranaike, in Sri Lanka, propagated Buddhist socialism in the mid-1950s, drawing their inspiration from Ashoka and Jayavarman VII. Leading contemporary Buddhist abbots considered U Nu to be an ideal Buddhist statesman in the Ashokan tradition.[14] Norodom Sihanouk, king of Cambodia for much of the twentieth century, linked himself to pre-colonial monarchy and Buddhism as two wheels of Dhamma, which for him had its origins in Ashoka's reign.[15] Sihanouk said, 'On the pillar which Emperor Ashoka had constructed for the edification of his subjects, one reads "I consider the well-being of all creatures as a goal for which I should fight".'[16]

Modern Times

In the wake of the euphoria and excitement of shedding colonial rule, virtually all of Buddhist Asia slid toward some form of dictatorship and/or civil strife. The countries that follow the Theravada Tradition (Sri Lanka and South East Asia), where historically Buddhist values suffused governance, have violated those values in the worst way. Sri Lanka and Myanmar are two extreme examples, but Cambodia has had the Khmer Rouge and Pol Pot, Laos had the Pathet Lao and Thailand has had a string of military dictatorships under its emasculated constitutional monarchy.

In Sri Lanka, although Prime Minister S.W.R.D. Bandaranaike (1956–1959) espoused Buddhist socialism, his government initiated an ethnic and a religious rift in the country by enacting The Official Language Act No. 33 of 1956, putting about thirty per cent of the population at a disadvantage in access to jobs. In 1971, the Universities Act provided preferences to ethnic Sinhala students for entrance to Sri Lankan universities; the next year, the new constitution recognised freedom of religion, but stipulated that the 'Republic of Sri Lanka shall give to Buddhism the foremost place, and accordingly it shall be the duty of the State to protect and foster Buddhism.' This clause politicised Buddhism and relegated Hinduism, Islam and Christianity to a lower status in the national consciousness.

The country's flag has evolved since its independence to include Buddhist, Hindu, and Muslim colours and symbols. In 1972, four Bodhi Tree leaves were added to represent loving kindness, compassion, equanimity and happiness. This symbolism was not enough to forestall twenty-six years of civil war, in which about 50,000 combatants and 100,000 civilians died, and hundreds of thousands (mainly Tamil Hindus and Muslims) were displaced. The cost of the war was estimated at $250 billion in 2009, about five times the country's GDP that year.

Almost ninety per cent of Myanmar's population is Buddhist, but its governance since the military took over in 1962 has been far from compassionate, despite regular media coverage of the merit-making activities of its top officials. The Bamar ethnic majority has sought to dominate ethnic minorities, especially the non-Buddhists, in the border areas, which are also rich in mineral resources. Internal conflict has been constant, with military operations to suppress insurgencies by the Karen, Kachin, Shan, Karenni and Rohingya people. The recent, and most brutal, military action was against the Muslim Rohingyas, leading to about 700,000 fleeing to Bangladesh when their villages were burned and people slaughtered. Buddhist Rohingyas initiated the violence. Sitagu Sayadaw, a senior and revered Buddhist monk, appeared to justify killing non-Buddhists by saying they were not fully human.

Mongolia and Bhutan, which follow the Tibetan Mahayana Tradition, have had better governance. As recently as the 1920s, Bogd Khan was both the religious and secular leader of Mongolia, while his brother was the chief abbot and advisor. The Stalinist purge in 1937 destroyed almost 700 monasteries; 30,000 monks were killed, and many more sent to gulags. But since 1990, Buddhism has enjoyed a rapid revival, and about eighty per cent of Mongolians now consider themselves Buddhists.

Bhutan took on its present shape in the seventeenth century. For about the next two centuries, it had Buddhist theocratic governance, a Dhammaraj, in which the civil leader was subordinate to the religious leader and the legal code for administrative, social and moral conduct was based on Buddhist Dharma. Although the country is now a democracy with a constitutional monarchy, its constitution confirms the traditional Chhoe-sid-nyi system of joint temporal and religious policy formulation. The Buddhist abbot, the religious head of the country, is the most powerful advisor to the civilian administration and king.

Buddha at Thimpu, Bhutan *(Photo courtesy: Ashok Khanna)*

Bhutan's constitution emphasises Buddhism as the spiritual heritage of the country, and seeks to promote peace, non-violence, compassion and tolerance. While poverty still exists, it is declining rapidly; Bhutan is easily the least corrupt country in South Asia. The government provides free education for all through the tenth standard and further for students who show aptitude. Women enjoy rights not available to them in neighbouring countries, such as a presumptive inheritance right of land ownership. Many marriages occur from choice rather than arrangement, and divorce is not uncommon. Unusually, the killing of animals is against the law in Bhutan, a very Ashokan piece of legislation, though meat imported from India is consumed. Bhutan's current legal code still retains a Buddhist foundation, and its environmental policies are notably progressive. The Bhutanese approach to governance is the closest I have come across in my travels to Ashoka's Dhammaraj.

Buddhism in the West

It is possible that Ashoka's emissaries to western kingdoms reached all the way to Egypt—Clement and Origen, early Alexandrian Fathers of the Christian church, refer to Buddhism. Certainly, contact between India, the Greek city-states and the Roman Empire is documented. Platonic doctrines such as the transmigration of souls could have come from India, Jewish and Christian monasticism and the cult of relics from Buddhism. Bruce Rich points to the similarity between Ashoka's Twelfth Major Rock Edict and the Epistle of Saint James, written in Syria about three centuries after Ashoka: both emphasise restraint of speech as an important basis for ethical and religious progress.

The first recorded encounter between European Christians and Buddhists was in 1253 CE, when the king of France sent William of Rubruck as an ambassador to the court of the Mongol Empire. Marco Polo also encountered Buddhism in the thirteenth century, during visits to Mongolia and Sri Lanka. He said that had the Buddha been a Christian, he would have been declared a great saint; a few centuries later, the Catholic Church did exactly that. In the seventeenth century, Buddhist Mongols established Kalmykia at the edge of Europe, the only Buddhist nation on the continent.

In 1844, the French philologist Eugene Burnouf determined that the religions practiced in many Asian countries were branches of a tradition that originated in India, laying the basis for Western studies of Buddhism. German philosopher Arthur Schopenhauer read about Buddhism and other Asian religions before devising his philosophical system; the American essayist Henry David Thoreau translated a Buddhist sutra from French into English. Friedrich Nietzsche praised Buddhism in his 1895 work, *The Anti-Christ*, calling it 'a hundred times more realistic than Christianity…. Buddhism makes no promises, but keeps them all.'

In the United States, The World Parliament of Religions, held in Chicago in 1893, was a pivotal event in the expansion of Buddhism. The Zen and Theravada traditions were especially well represented, with delegates arriving from India, Japan, Thailand, China and Sri Lanka. Buddhism was presented as the most scientific of all religions, not based on faith, with doctrines that could be tested through experience. Waves of Chinese, Japanese and South East Asian migration also brought Buddhist traditions to American soil, spawning strong institutions that have flourished up to today. American interest in the twentieth century was initially focused on Zen literature, which influenced writers like the Beat novelist Jack Kerouac.

The lay Buddhist tradition Vipassana (which means 'insight' in Pali) became especially popular in the latter half of the twentieth century through the teaching of the Indian industrialist Satya Narayan Goenka, who was born in Myanmar and became a leader of the Hindu community there. The Goenka student William Hart states that Goenka was part of a heritage of 'traditional teachers who had preserved it through generations since ancient times, when the teaching of the Buddha was first introduced to Burma,'[17] which of course happened because of Ashoka's initiative. From his headquarters in Mumbai, Goenka established Vipassana centres around the world.

Western Buddhism has become more and more distinctive. It is predominantly a lay practice, tends to eschew traditional Buddhist hierarchy, is increasingly non-sexist and is not rigidly sectarian, allowing for a great deal of exchange between Vipassana, Zen and Tibetan teachers and practitioners. Today, Buddhism has about four million followers in North America and 1.5 million in Europe; it is the fastest growing religion in Australia.

Thousands of years later, Dhamma lives on through these practices. It is truly remarkable what Ashoka has given to the world.

Post-Independence India

How has India, after Independence, fared in regard to Ashoka's principles of non-violence, tolerance and public good?

Constitution

Apparently, Prime Minister Nehru was obsessed with Ashoka. As a student, he carried a version of Ashoka's inscriptions in his satchel, and later he gave his daughter Indira the feminine version of one of Ashoka's titles as her middle name (Piyadasini). Nehru admired Ashoka's non-violence, his secular approach and his diligent and considerate administration. He pushed hard to immortalise Ashoka by ensuring that the emperor's chakra (wheel of law) and lion capital were incorporated in India's National Flag and seal. 'In Jawaharlal Nehru,' wrote Amaury De Riencourt, 'India has found a remarkable reincarnation of Emperor Asoka.' Lahiri holds that Gandhi's belief in non-violence was derived from Ashoka, as well. Gandhi looked to the emperor in reviving his political value system, and for moral energy in the struggle for independence.[18]

Before the Indian Constitution was written, the Congress Party (at the initiative of Nehru and Gandhi) drafted a resolution on the rights of minorities that stressed India would be 'a democratic, secular state, where all citizens enjoy full rights and are equally entitled to the protection of the State, irrespective of the religion to which they belong.' In his first major speech to the Constituent Assembly in December 1946, before India's Independence, Nehru proclaimed that India as a sovereign republic would guarantee its citizens 'justice, social, economic and political; equality of status; of opportunity; and before the law; freedom of thought, expression, belief, faith, worship, vocation, association and action, subject to law and public morality.' In moving the resolution, he invoked the 'great past of India... as well as modern precedents such as the French, American and Russian Revolutions.'

While it's not possible to disentangle the influence of Ashoka from that of modern liberal democracy, the coincidence of values is remarkable. Perhaps Nehru's greatest achievement in modern India, following Ashoka's tradition, was creating a secular state in a religious country and granting equal rights to untouchables. In this effort, he was supported by Dr B.R. Ambedkar, the first minister of law of India, chairman of the Constitution Drafting Committee, for whom the challenge was ensuring equal citizenship in a highly unequal society, riven by caste, class and religious differences. Ambedkar, who was from a low caste, believed that the Buddhist Dharma was the only religious doctrine that could be reconciled fully with modern science and the political values of liberty and equality. He converted to Buddhism late in his life, together with several hundred thousand of his low caste brethren.

Here are some salient excerpts from India's Constitution:

Fundamental Rights

Article 14: The State shall not deny to any person equality before the law or the equal protection of the laws within the territory of India.

Article 15: The State shall not discriminate against any citizen on grounds only of religion, race, caste, sex, place of birth or any of them.

Article16: There shall be equality of opportunity for all citizens in matters relating to employment or appointment to any office under the State.

Article 17: 'Untouchability' is abolished and its practice in any form is forbidden.

The enforcement of any disability arising out of 'Untouchability' shall be an offence punishable in accordance with law.

Article 19: All citizens shall have the right—
(a) to freedom of speech and expression;
(b) to assemble peaceably and without arms;
(c) to form associations or unions;
(d) to move freely throughout the territory of India;
(e) to reside and settle in any part of the territory of India; and
(f) to practice any profession, or to carry on any occupation, trade
*   or business.*

Article 25: Subject to public order, morality and health and to
the other provisions of this Part, all persons are equally entitled
to freedom of conscience and the right freely to profess, practice and
propagate religion.

Directives of State Policy

The provisions contained in this Part shall not be enforceable by
any court, but the principles therein laid down are nevertheless
fundamental in the governance of the country and it shall be the
duty of the State to apply these principles in making laws.

Article 38:
(1) The State shall strive to promote the welfare of the people by
securing and protecting as effectively as it may a social order in
which justice, social, economic and political, shall inform all the
institutions of the national life.
(2) The State shall, in particular, strive to minimise the inequalities
in income, and endeavour to eliminate inequalities in status,
facilities and opportunities, not only amongst individuals but also
amongst groups of people residing in different areas or engaged in
different vocations.

Article 39: The State shall, in particular, direct its policy towards securing—

(a) that the citizens, men and women equally, have the right to an adequate means of livelihood;

(b) that the ownership and control of the material resources of the community are so distributed as best to subserve the common good;

(c) that the operation of the economic system does not result in the concentration of wealth and means of production to the common detriment;

(d) that there is equal pay for equal work for both men and women;

(e) that the health and strength of workers, men and women, and the tender age of children are not abused and that citizens are not forced by economic necessity to enter avocations unsuited to their age or strength; and

(f) that children are given opportunities and facilities to develop in a healthy manner and in conditions of freedom and dignity and that childhood and youth are protected against exploitation and against moral and material abandonment.

Article 39A: The State shall secure that the operation of the legal system promotes justice, on a basis of equal opportunity, and shall, in particular, provide free legal aid, by suitable legislation or schemes or in any other way, to ensure that opportunities for securing justice are not denied to any citizen by reason of economic or other disabilities.

Secular Democracy

A report by the Pew Research Center analyses the extent of impingement on religious beliefs in 198 countries in two parts: the government restrictions index assesses government policies that restrict religious beliefs and practices; and the social hostilities index measures acts by private individuals and groups, including religious sectarian violence. India ranks fourth from the bottom in the social hostilities index, a little better than Iraq, Nigeria and Syria. Among the world's twenty-five most populous countries, Russia, Egypt, India, Pakistan and Nigeria stand out as having the most restrictions on religion (as of the end of 2015) when both government and social hostilities are taken into account.

Violence

While in per capita measures the level of violence in India may seem to have attenuated in recent years, underreporting is substantial, and by any measure the sheer numbers are startling. Triggers for violence include religious, caste, class, cultural and gender differences—often several of these factors combine to create trouble.

By far the greatest casualties occurred during the partition of colonial India into the nations of India and Pakistan. Gandhi was unable to prevent the massive violence between Muslims and Hindus that followed, and paid with his life for his efforts. Estimates are vague, but the number of people killed was between one and two million. When the dust settled, 7.3 million refugees had to resettle in India, according to the 1951 Census.

During the Independence period, in 1947, my family lived in a house in Delhi divided into two flats. Because we could hear gunfire and tanks a couple of miles away, in a more congested neighbourhood, the entire household slept on the roof. The two fathers, armed with rifles, took turns patrolling after dark. Being amateurs, they were not alert to three killings just outside our house one night. The next day, all the women and children moved to a friend's house thought to be in a safer area, near a Sikh temple. On our very first night there, the temple was attacked, and dead bodies were discovered the next morning littering the grounds. On the way back to our flat the next day, we passed Connaught Place, the ritzy shopping area of Delhi. Looters were busy breaking into shops and taking whatever they could carry.

The ripples of Partition have continued through to the present with border skirmishes, wars in 1964–1965 and 1971, a serious conflict in Kargil in 1999, and several terrorist attacks with a total cost of about 30,000 lives through 2016, according to the Global Terrorism database.

Within India, although the Constitution aspired to include diverse people that spoke different languages and practiced a variety of religions, this level of unity had not taken hold at Independence. The geographic area of India had not been under one government since Ashoka—the British ruled a substantial portion of the country indirectly, through more than 500 supposedly independent rulers. Unsurprisingly, several secessionist and extremist movements erupted after 1947, based on religious, cultural and class differences. There are no estimates of casualties available for the Nagaland and Mizoram separatist conflicts in the North East, but the Sikh secessionist movement cost between 20,000 and 70,000 lives,[19] and the Kashmir Independence movement cost 28,500 lives.[20] The Naxalite (Communist/Maoist) revolutionary movement, which still operates in a huge swath of the country, has cost about 14,000 lives. In addition to the killing, which has fallen heavily on civilians, security forces have been accused of human rights abuses in all of these cases.

Random incendiary incidents have also sparked religious violence, such as the killing of about 3,000 Sikhs after Prime Minister Indira Gandhi's assassination by her Sikh bodyguard in 1984. Two thousand people were killed when the Babri Masjid was torn down in a fit of religious fervour in 1992. And in 2002, another 2,000 died in Gujarat when Muslims were suspected of killing some Hindus on a train. Sadly, the list of deaths does not end with public conflicts. Domestic security is lax, especially for the poor and in rural areas. In 2016, a study conducted by the United Nations Office on Drugs and Crime cited India as having the largest number of reported murders in the world, at 30,450 (China had 8,634).

Violence against women is also rampant in India. The National Crime Records Bureau Report recorded 38,947 cases of rape in 2016 and 7,621 cases of 'dowry deaths' in 2017. A 2018 poll by Thomson Reuters of 548 experts on women's issues ranked India as the most dangerous country in the world for women. The parameters considered were healthcare, discrimination, cultural traditions, sexual and non-sexual violence, and human trafficking. India ranked worst in sexual violence and harassment. Reported crimes against women rose by eighty-three per cent between 2007 and 2016.

Governance

The fruitfulness of all human activities relies ultimately on effective governance.[21] In modern terms, this includes the process by which governments are selected, monitored and replaced; their capacity to formulate and implement good policies; and the respect shown by the government and citizens for political and social institutions. The World Bank aggregates data from about fifteen surveys on six specific aspects of governance— accountability, political stability, effectiveness, regulatory quality, rule of law and corruption.[22] In the 2016 survey results,

India improved its position in the past decade to 111 from 124 out of 214 countries. Its rise, though, was because of an improvement in the control of corruption; all other categories remained stable or worsened. It has a particularly poor standing in political stability and rule of law, ranking 181.

Politics and Administration

Over the decades, political parties in India have become family firms. The most prominent example is the Congress Party and the Nehru dynasty, with Nehru, Indira Gandhi and Rajiv Gandhi having served as prime ministers, Sonia Gandhi served as the President of the Congress Party, and Rahul Gandhi contested the last election. In sixty-six years of post-independence rule, prime ministers from the Nehru family have held the office for nearly four decades between them. This practice has been extended down the system, to sons and daughters being nominated to parliament if the sitting member dies. By one estimate, nearly thirty per cent of the members of parliament come from political families. Indeed, all MPs under the age of thirty, and almost two-thirds between the ages of thirty-one and forty, were found to be hereditary. Many state political parties are dynastic, as well, with several clan members represented in state assemblies, dominating politics for decades and enriching themselves as a result.[23]

Not only is nepotism rife in the political class, but so is criminal behaviour and corruption. The Parliament elected in 2014 had the highest number of elected members with criminal charges to date. A 2014 report by the Association for Democratic Reforms showed thirty-four per cent of the lower house of India's Parliament had criminal cases pending; almost two-thirds of those cases were for serious crimes.

In one state legislature, the figure was fifty-seven per cent. Even if convicted of misdeeds, many elected representatives walk away scot-free, and sometimes get elected yet again. A Gallup survey of sixty countries found that the lack of confidence in politicians was highest in India, where ninety-one per cent of those polled felt that their elected representatives were dishonest.

Administration, meanwhile, is corrupt, inefficient and ineffective. In a 2009 survey of the leading Asian economies, India's bureaucracy was rated the least efficient and most painfully slow to work with; a 2012 study by Political and Economic Risk Consultancy said the quality of Indian bureaucracy is the worst in Asia. Businesses complain about inadequate infrastructure and corruption requiring companies to make under-the-table payments to overcome bureaucratic inertia and gain official favours in India. Transparency International estimates that truckers pay about $4.5 billion annually in bribe at state border crossings.

Corruption

India ranked 81 out of 180 countries in Transparency International's Corruption Perceptions Index for 2017, an improvement from the prior few years' surveys. But the ranking does not capture the insidious corruption that permeates every aspect of daily life in India. A study by professors Bibek Debroy and Laveesh Bhandari claims that officials extort about 1.25 per cent of GDP annually. That may be an underestimate, as the normal kickback on contracts, especially large defence deals, is twenty per cent. India's Planning Commission estimated that seventy to ninety per cent of Indian rural development funds are siphoned off.

Some estimates suggest that India has more black money than the rest of the world combined, and that $1.4 trillion of it has found its way into Swiss bank deposits. Another study by Global Financial Integrity disputes this amount, and calculates the loss as merely $460 billion (in 2010 dollars) in the period from 1948 to 2008. Legislation such as the Prevention of Corruption and Right to Information Acts have had little effect, as the conviction rate has been ridiculously low, partly because the judicial system is also corrupt.

Despite the bleak picture, there is hope. The latest India Corruption Study found that the proportion of Indians who felt that corruption had increased in the previous year fell from seventy per cent in 2005 to forty-five per cent in 2010. Also, recent public outcry has resulted in the passage of a bill to establish an independent anti-corruption agency.

Poverty and Inequality

The World Bank's snapshot of India in 2010 shows that about one in five Indians is poor—a staggering 270 million people. This estimate is at the lower end of the measures, which go all the way up to over seventy per cent of the population. South Asia as a whole is home to just under half of the world's poor people. Gandhi said that poverty is the worst kind of violence.

To be sure, poverty has declined since Independence, but that decline has slowed in recent decades. Inequality has worsened since 1991, when major market-oriented economic reforms began to open India's economy to the world. In 2017, the wealthiest one per cent owned fifty-eight per cent of India's wealth, and captured seventy-three per cent of the increase in the nation's wealth in that year.

Women's participation in the workforce in India remains extremely low by international standards. In the G20 countries, only Saudi Arabia has a lower rate. Pervasive violence against women inhibits increased involvement. Just two out of twenty-three Supreme Court judges are women, and their share of seats in parliament and state legislatures has not exceeded about ten per cent. Eighty-four per cent of participants in a survey in 2012 concluded that men have more right to work than women when jobs are scarce.

Legislation banning caste discrimination and affirmative action programmes to assist lower castes and women has ameliorated the situation somewhat, but not much. Caste continues to be the crux of inequality in modern India. The system has oppressed the majority of its population since centuries before Ashoka's time. His effort to treat people equally has not yet taken hold. Upper caste men still dominate corporate boards, judicial institutions, the media and land ownership. The discontent among the landless rural poor sparked a powerful armed rebellion by the Naxalites, who remain active in nine states.

Conclusion

While the Indian Constitution's Fundamental Rights and Directives of State Policy are consonant with Ashokan and modern liberal democratic values, their implementation leaves much to be desired. Greater awareness—and amelioration—of the plight of hundreds of millions of socially and politically oppressed people is needed. Unfortunately, the increasing concentration of wealth and power stands in the way.

The recreation of Nalanda University is a ray of hope that Ashokan values will live on. A consortium of Asian countries including India has raised funds to build a residential university in Bihar, not far from the site of its ancient Buddhist predecessor. It began its first student session in 2014.

Ruins of the ancient Nalanda University *(Photo courtesy: Ashok Khanna)*

There is also Ashoka University in Sonipat, near Delhi. It aims to provide world-class education and prepare students 'to be ethical leaders in a diverse and complex world, the kind envisioned by Emperor Ashoka 2,000 years ago.' The historian Nayanjot Lahiri now teaches there.

The Ashoka Foundation in Mumbai, founded in 1995, is dedicated to encouraging 'charitable and social service activities of every kind to help the needy and poor sections of society.' Its mission is 'to create political, economic, educational and social systems that promote peace, human welfare and the sustainability of the environment on which life depends.'

An international non-profit organisation called Ashoka, based in the Washington, D.C. area, was founded by Bill Drayton in 1980 to promote social entrepreneurship—a term he coined—around the world. He named the organisation after

Ashoka; Drayton's vision was to encourage people to creatively and ethically make changes for the good of society. He had learned about the exemplary emperor when he visited India at the age of nineteen. Later, at Harvard, he created the Ashoka Table, bringing in prominent government, union and church leaders for off-the-record dinners at which students could ask 'how things really worked'. His organisation has offices and activities all over the world, including in India.

India's democracy is still young. Its roots are deepening, and its sinews are strengthening. The lower castes, who are the majority of the population and a still greater majority of the poor, are now asserting their rights through elections. The women's movement is gathering steam. A glimmer of hope remains that modern India can still become the non-violent, tolerant and compassionate society that Ashoka once tried to create.

CHAPTER 8

Legendary Ashoka

Since many readers may well be interested in knowing the vital details of what the Northern and Southern legends say about Ashoka, I will provide here an account of how he was known for the centuries before the edicts were understood, once again. It should be kept in mind that legends are primarily mythologised stories told with religious motivation; they cannot be counted on to reflect historical reality, except when confirmed through other ways. Most scholars, though, believe that at least some elements of them could be accurate.

As with many great ancient narratives—ranging from the Mahabharata to the story of King David, in the Hebrew Bible—the Ashokan legends surely originated in oral traditions that were eventually written down and collected. Studies have shown that storytellers in ancient times could remember and recite massive amounts of material, blending historical and mythological elements.

The Northern collection—the *Asokavadana*—dates from the second century CE, and incorporates accounts of Ashoka from the north eastern regions of his empire, where Buddhism has flourished ever since his time. It was written in Sanskrit.

It opens by celebrating the prior-life saintliness of Upagupta, whom it credits as Ashoka's mentor on all spiritual matters, and as his guide on his protracted pilgrimage to Buddhist sites. This opening signals the work's primary aim: showing how Buddhist elders in the Mahayana Tradition sought to control the emperor's violence, and direct him toward support of the Buddhist community and its message. The text describes Ashoka meeting the Buddha in his previous life, when he was a little boy named Jaya who offered the Buddha a handful of dirt that he gratefully accepted, telling the boy that he would be reborn as Ashoka a hundred years after the Buddha's death.

The *Asokavadana* names Subhadrangi, daughter of a Brahman, as Ashoka's mother; she manoeuvres to become King Bindusara's primary queen by first endearing herself to him as his barber. She chooses the name Ashoka, meaning 'without sorrow', because his birth freed her from suffering. But Bindusara rejects the boy, whose skin is 'rough and unpleasant to the touch'. A fortune-teller nevertheless avows that Ashoka will be enthroned as emperor in due course.

When Ashoka is in his teens, his father sends him to Taxila to settle a restive situation, and probably to isolate him from the court. Ashoka successfully mollifies the city without resort to violence, and continues to impress the king's officials, especially minister Radhagupta. He is sent next to Ujjain to administer the territory there; along the way, in the nearby city of Vidisha, he meets Devi, the daughter of a prominent merchant. They begin cohabiting in Ujjain, and have two children.

Ashoka is said to have befriended Greek mercenaries in the northwest, who are eventually credited with aiding him in his attainment of the throne. Meanwhile, the heir-apparent crown prince, Sushima, is reported to have insulted the emperor's chief minister by slapping his bald head in jest. The chief minister fears that Sushima would be just as reckless as emperor, and persuades his fellow ministers, including his son Radhagupta, to block Sushima's ascension in favour of Ashoka. When the Taxilans rise in rebellion again, Emperor Bindusara sends Sushima to deal with the insurrection; the emperor then falls ill and recalls Sushima, ordering Ashoka to go in his place. But the ministers delay the imperial order and smear Ashoka's body with red turmeric so that he appears too sick to travel. When it is clear that Bindusara is dying, Ashoka dons full imperial regalia and appears before his father to request that he be declared temporary emperor. The encounter enrages Bindusara so much that he throws up blood and dies.

When Sushima learns of his father's death, he marches toward Pataliputra. Ashoka is said to have deployed his Greek mercenary allies to guard two of the city's gates, with Radhagupta and Ashoka arranging protection of a third and fourth. Here is John Strong's translation of the relevant *Asokavadana* text: 'Radhagupta set up an artificial elephant, on top of which he placed an image of Ashoka that he had fashioned. All around, he dug up a ditch. He filled it with live coals of acacia wood, covered it with weeds and camouflaged it all with dirt. He then went and taunted Sushima [sic]: "If you are able to kill Ashoka, you will become king." Sushima immediately rushed to the eastern gate, intending to engage in a battle with his half-brother, but he fell into the ditch full of charcoal, and came to an untimely and painful end.' Ashoka is also said to have had his other brothers, who might have threatened his ascension, assassinated.

After his accession to the throne, a chapter titled *Chandashoka* evidently meant to stress his nefarious character prior to his conversion to Buddhism—relates that when Ashoka's ministers challenge his order to cut down all fruit and flowering trees, he has 500 of them beheaded. (Round numbers, such as 500, were a common exaggeration in legends. The story also reflects the *Arthasastra's* advice that the emperor should test the loyalty of ministers by giving them unlikely challenges.) When Ashoka sees that his concubines don't want to caress his rough skin, he has hundreds of them burnt to death as well. Further, he is said to have built a prison, called Ashoka's hell, where he appoints the 'fierce mountaineer' Chandragirika as his executioner, allowing him and his underlings free reign to torture and kill the prison's inmates.

The *Asokavadana* credits Ashoka's conversion to Buddhism to his encounter with the saintly young monk Samudra, who wanders into the prison begging for alms and is severely tortured without ever losing his serenity. Samudra reveals to Ashoka that he has been liberated from 'the terrors of *samsara*—the suffering engendered by rebirth—because of the teachings of the Buddha.' He tells Ashoka that the Buddha foretold that one hundred years after his death, a great emperor named Ashoka will appear. The monarch will be a *chakravartin*, a 'wheel-turning ruler', who will be a civil counterpart to the turning of the wheel of Dharma by the Buddha in the spiritual realm. He will also be a *Dharmaraja*, a righteous king, who will spread the Buddha's relics far and wide throughout his realm in 84,000 *dharmarajikas*—righteous-ruler monuments known as stupas. Samudra tells him that this is his true destiny.

Ashoka is so moved by the monk's serenity that he converts to Buddhism and has the prison destroyed. He adopts the elder monk Upagupta as his spiritual guide, and proceeds to atone for his past sins by committing to building the prophesied stupas at renowned Buddhist sites throughout his empire. Upagupta takes Ashoka on a pilgrimage to the stupas of great Buddhist saints; Ashoka is especially struck by the dire condition of the

Bodhi Tree in Bodh Gaya. He is told that the Bodhi Tree was cursed by Tishyarakshita, his chief queen, because she was upset about Ashoka's abandonment of their traditional religion. The queen duly acknowledges her misdeed, has the curse removed, and orders the tree be refreshed with a 1,000 pitchers of milk until it revives. Ashoka subsequently commands that a huge Buddhist festival be celebrated outside of Pataliputra every five years thereafter. He invites monks from all over the empire to attend, and appoints an elder to spread the truth of the Buddha's Dharma throughout the realm.

The *Asokavadana* next relates the birth of Ashoka's son Dharmavivardhana by his queen Padmavati. The emperor is struck by the beauty of the baby's eyes; when he hears them compared to a Himalayan bird, he gives the boy a new name, Kunala. A Buddhist elder predicts that Kunala will become blind, thereby reinforcing the truth that nothing is permanent in life.

The dark lady of the Northern Tradition, the chief queen Tishyarakshita, again enters the picture. She falls in love with Kunala's striking looks, but Kunala spurns her advances, prompting Tishyarakshita to seek revenge against him. In a story obviously imitative of Ashoka's youthful assignment as vice regal envoy, Kunala is then dispatched to Taxila to quell another rebellion. Like his father, he is well received in Taxila, but back in the capital Ashoka's health starts to fail precipitously, with something impure secreting from his pores. Kunala is recalled to Pataliputra to rule the empire, but Queen Tishyarakshita fears that he will have her assassinated if he takes the throne. Seeking a cure for Ashoka's illness, she finds someone with similar symptoms and has him killed so that the body can be examined. A tapeworm is discovered in the man's stomach; various methods are attempted to kill the worm, but none succeed until an onion does the job. The queen has Ashoka treated with an onion, and he recovers. As a reward, she asks him to allow her to rule the empire for a week. He agrees, and she then exacts her revenge against Kunala, dispatching an order in Ashoka's name directing that the prince's eyes be gouged out.

Submitting to his preordained fate, Kunala is blinded. He and his wife become beggar musicians, and make their way toward Pataliputra. Ashoka soon hears someone singing outside the palace walls, and has the singer invited in. When the king recognises Kunala, he falls down and breaks into tears. Hearing what has happened, he commands that Queen Tishyarakshita be seized and tortured to death. But Kunala pleads for the queen to be forgiven, and due to this act of compassion he is miraculously able to see again. Ashoka, though, despite forgiving her as requested, still has the queen burned to death.

Afterward, Ashoka introduces his younger brother Vitashoka to Buddhist teachings. Eventually Vitashoka becomes a monk, and takes up residency in the Cock monastery outside Pataliputra. After a while, finding the place too noisy, he sets out for the Himalayas. One day, a cowherd mistakes him for a man who had insulted the image of the Buddha, and thereby earned Ashoka's condemnation; Vitashoka is killed, and the cowherd brings his head to the king to claim his reward. Ashoka recognises his brother, and is grief-stricken. Upagupta tells him that his brother's fate resulted from the monarch's cruelty.

Showing increasing signs of ageing and failing health, Ashoka dedicates his remaining energy to giving away his wealth to the Buddhist *Sangha*. His donations threaten the empire with bankruptcy; Prince Sampadi, Kunala's son and heir apparent to the throne, consults with his advisors and orders the state treasurer not to give away anything more. Ashoka then proceeds to give away his personal possessions instead, and ends up with only half of a cherry plum fruit. Dying, he donates the fruit to the Cock monastery, where it is mashed and put into the monks' soup. In his last moments, he asks his chief minister Radhagupta to reassure him that he is still the ruler of the world. Then, with dramatic gestures, he declares that he is presenting the whole earth to the Buddhist community. He has the declaration written down, seals it and dies. The ministers of the empire manage to use its remaining resources to get the imperial holdings back from the *Sangha,* and Sampadi is confirmed as the new ruler. A kind of afterword relates how the last Mauryan emperor Pushyamitra, several generations after Ashoka's death, destroyed all the vestiges of Buddhism in India—monasteries and stupas, among others. The old religion of the Brahmans once again becomes dominant.

The southern legend collection, the *Mahavamsa,* or the 'Great Dynastic Chronicle', dates from the fifth century CE, and expands on an earlier fourth century CE collection, the *Dipavamsa*—the 'Island Chronicle', described by George Turnour as 'the principal historical record in Ceylon… from BCE 543 to CE 301.' The *Mahavamsa* relates the rise of Buddhism in Sri Lanka, and contains accounts of Ashoka as a crucial part of that history. It provides the earliest known account of the life of the Buddha, and thereafter uses a double dating system based on the Buddha's death and the enthronement of each ruler. The system provides probable dates for the first three Mauryan emperors, and especially for Ashoka. As we highlighted earlier, the text also allows us to identify Ashoka as Piyadasi, 'beloved of the gods', the name he uses in his edicts.

The *Mahavamsa* recounts the overthrow of Dhana Nanda, the last emperor in the Nanda line, by the Brahman minister Chanakya, who then installs Ashoka's grandfather Chandragupta as the new ruler. Chandragupta rules for twenty-four years, and his son Bindusara rules for twenty-eight. Bindusara is said to have had one hundred and one sons, by different mothers; Ashoka emerges as all-powerful because of his faith and wisdom, and by arranging for his hundred brothers to be killed off. The chronicle gives the date of Ashoka's ascension to the throne as two hundred and eighteen years after the death of the Buddha, approximately 269 BCE.

Like the *Asokavadana*, the *Mahavamsa* relates the story of Ashoka being sent as viceroy to govern the kingdom of Avanti from its capital, Ujjain. (It adds that he was sent because of a rumour that he was going to have his father killed, and usurp the throne.) It too tells of Ashoka stopping at Vidisha and meeting and marrying 'a lovely maiden named Devi', the daughter of a merchant. They have 'a beautiful boy' named Mahinda, and, two years later, a daughter named Sanghamitta. Since the Northern and Southern traditions give virtually the same story, it seems to be a reliable one.

Ten years later, Ashoka learns that his father is dying, and rushes to Pataliputra. As soon as his father dies, he takes control of the capital and has his older brother, the heir-apparent (here called Sumana), killed, thereby making himself the logical successor. However, it takes four years before he secures enough power to be enthroned. The chronicle doesn't reconcile this story with the earlier one about Ashoka killing one hundred brothers and thereby attaining the throne, but its account of Ashoka arranging the death of his older brother dovetails with the story in the *Asokavadana*.

Ashoka names his younger brother Tissa (Vitashoka, in the *Asokavadana*), son of the same mother, as his primary viceroy. He gains a reputation for violence, and is referred to as *Chandashoka*. But because of the revolting behaviour of the Brahmans at the palace, who insist on being supported by the realm while practicing animal sacrifice and other rituals, he starts to have doubts about continuing his father's devotion to 'the Brahmanical faith'. Ashoka orders leaders of all religions to meet him and discuss the essence of their faiths. He is struck by the serenity of a young Buddhist monk named Nigrodha, the orphaned son of Sumana, the brother he had killed. Ashoka queries him about Buddhist teachings, and becomes convinced that Buddhism is the true faith.

Ashoka becomes a lay Buddhist, bans the Brahmans from his court, and replaces them with Buddhist monks. The head monk—here also named Tissa—becomes Ashoka's mentor and primary guide throughout his life. Again, as in the *Asokavadana*, Ashoka is instructed to build 84,000 stupas and monasteries, here specified as honouring the 84,000 discourses on the tenets of Buddhism. He orders the building of a monastery called Ashokarama (rather than the Cock monastery, as in the *Asokavadana*) just outside the capital. The building of monasteries takes three years, and he has a huge festival to honour their completion, making large donations to the Buddhist *Sangha*. On the day of the festival at Ashokarama, he is honoured as *Dharmashoka*, Ashoka of the Dharma, forever changing his Fierce Ashoka designation.

Tissa then urges Ashoka to have his children Mahinda and Sanghamitta become Buddhist monks. The children do so, as does his younger brother Tissa, six years after Ashoka became emperor. Buddhism thrives within the realm, but factions emerge, each advocating conflicting doctrines. After seven years of this conflict, Ashoka realises that he needs to intervene. He summons his mentor from a long retreat in the Himalayas and convenes an assembly of the monastic community in what is later known as the Third Buddhist Council. The event is reported to have lasted nine months, in the seventeenth year of Ashoka's rule; eventually, 60,000 monks are expelled for heresy. Ashoka's mentor Tissa directs the remaining monks in establishing the teachings of true Dharma.

The chronicle then shifts back to Sri Lanka, where Devanamapiyatissa ('Tissa, Beloved-of-the-Gods') becomes king. He decides to send some of the crown jewels to Ashoka, who responds with his own gifts. Ashoka also advises the Sri Lankan king to take refuge in the Buddha and to guide his people in that path, as he has.

Tissa the head monk, who has routinely sent Buddhist missionaries to every part of the empire, sends to Sri Lanka a delegation of five monks, led by Ashoka's son Mahinda. Prior to his departure, Mahinda goes to Vidisha to see his mother Devi, who has become a Buddhist nun herself at a monastery on a hill outside the city (where Ashoka later has the magnificent Sanchi stupa built). Mahinda's party, now including his sister and her son, is then said to have flown to a mountaintop in Sri Lanka. The missionaries are received warmly by King Devanamapiyatissa, who converts to Buddhism along with his family and his palace.

Mahinda then dispatches his son Sumana to Pataliputra to obtain relics of the Buddha. Sumana, finding Ashoka worshipping at the Bodhi tree, receives the Buddha's alms bowl from his grandfather and proceeds to the Himalayas, where two other major relics are retrieved. These are sent to Sri Lanka, where King Devanamapiyatissa has a huge stupa built to contain them.

Through his daughter Sanghamitta, who has become a nun in the Sri Lankan Buddhist community, Devanamapiyatissa asks Ashoka for a branch of the Bodhi Tree. After great deliberation, Ashoka oversees an elaborate ceremony at the end of which a cutting is taken from the tree, potted, and sent downriver and on to Sri Lanka, after yet another seaside ritual that concludes with the emperor wading into deep water to personally place the cutting on board. Ashoka is said to have sobbed with grief as he viewed the branch leaving for the island.

King Devanamapiyatissa has the cutting planted in his royal garden, and goes on to follow Ashoka's example in having stupas and monasteries built all over his realm. The chronicle thus shows that Ashoka was greatly responsible for the spread of Buddhism to Sri Lanka, where it has flourished ever since, long after its decline in India.

The rest of the *Mahavamsa* says nothing further about him, except to relate the story of his conflict with his evil queen, who complains about his consuming devotion to the Bodhi Tree and tries to have it killed with poison. It elegiacally reports that he died four years later, his ability to further champion Buddhism having already diminished.

Another text, *The History of Buddhism in India*, attributed to Tibetan Lama Taranatha, was discovered in 1840; it features three chapters about Ashoka. Although the woodblock-printed book seems to date back only to 1608, it draws on older sources. Scholars regard its account as unreliable, but its early stories may reflect historical reminiscences.

Taranatha credits not Upagupta but Yasha, head of the Cock monastery and also mentioned in the *Mahavamsa*, as Ashoka's teacher and advisor. Ashoka is presented as having led a dissolute life in his early years, before his mission to Taxila and the elimination of his brothers. He is again said to have been ruthlessly cruel at the start of his reign; soon, though, as in the *Asokavadana*, he encounters a young monk in his hellish prison who survives the experience with no ill effects. Yasha, the youth's guru, in due course convinces Ashoka to become a Buddhist, thereby transforming the ruler's story from one of consuming evil to one of ardent faith and good deeds. Yasha convenes a month-long festival of tens of thousands of monks from far and wide that takes place in a huge centre that Ashoka has built. Thereafter, Ashoka proceeds to expand his empire through the power of non-violent persuasion, collecting relics and building stupas for them throughout his realm.

Taranatha also tells the story of Ashoka's son Kunala being blinded, but here Kunala's blindness is said to have disqualified him as heir-apparent; he becomes a monk instead. Another son, here called Vigatashoka, is declared to be his father's successor. Taranatha's account concludes by describing how the emperor declined in power and virtue, and died without escaping rebirth.

When the India-and-environs travelogues of the Chinese Buddhist monks Faxian (fifth century CE) and Xuanzang (seventh century CE) were translated in the nineteenth century, scholars were enthused to rediscover the lost story of Buddhist India. Faxian's fifteen-year pilgrimage was the result of the rise of Buddhism in China. Inspired to meet the demand for copies and translations of texts from the Indian realm, he left China in 399 CE, recording his experiences and discoveries in *A Record of the Buddhistic Kingdoms.* During his travels, he encountered two stupas that he learned had been built by a regional king, Kinisha. He also heard about a ruler of a much larger empire centuries earlier whom Kinisha greatly admired and modelled himself after, through benign governance and support for Buddhism.

This great emperor was already known in China as Wuyou Wang, 'The King Not Feeling Sorrow'. He was revered among Chinese Buddhists as a 'wheel-turning ruler', a secular counterpart to the Buddha. Faxian tells the story of King Wuyou as a boy in a previous life meeting the Buddha and offering dirt for his begging bowl. He says that that good deed resulted in Wuyou returning as a ruler of the iron wheel and sovereign over India.

Faxian heard about this great ruler throughout his travels. He learned of non-Buddhist Indian rulers who still followed Wuyou's *Dhamma* regime, ruling with care and promoting civility and compassion in their realms, as well as supporting Buddhism. He even found Brahmanical sovereigns who were tolerant of all religions, surely also a heritage of Ashoka's rule.

Faxian subsequently learned that King Wuyou had founded a monastery at the site of the Buddha's death, and erected a giant image of the Buddha. He saw a tall pillar with a lion on top and inscriptions below that were also credited to Wuyou. Eventually, he made his way to Pataliputra, which he knew had been the city from where King Wuyou ruled his empire. There he saw the grand palace, large halls, impressive wooden walls and gates, and more large stupas. A stupa outside the city had two columns with inscriptions nearby, and one had a lion on top. He stayed for three years at the monastery that Wuyou had built outside the city.

Because of Faxian's journal, India gained a reputation among the Chinese as a Buddhist Shangri-La, where great wheel-turning rulers governed as *dharmarajas*. Xuanzang inherited this view of India as the true source of Buddhist teaching; he was inspired to journey west in 629 CE. Traveling along the Silk Road, via Samarkand and Bokhara, he discovered the first cache of scriptures that eventually became part of the massive collection he assembled. In modern-day Pakistan, he learned of a Buddhist king who treated the people of his realm with love and concern, very much in the spirit of Wuyou. However, from his perspective, the king's territory had become a desolate landscape of Buddhism in decline, with Brahmanism on the rise. Outside the ruined city of Taxila, he came across several stupas credited to Ashoka, including one said to be at the site where Kunala's eyes had been gouged out.

In Kashmir, where he was hosted by its Buddhist ruler, Xuanzang sees stupas and monasteries established by King Wuyou, and a seventy-foot pillar erected by the legendary king. He describes it as shiny, with inscriptions all around, and a lion on its top, ready to pounce.

Later, at Kannouj, Xuanzang meets yet another king, Harsha the Great, ruling according to Ashokan principles. He sees more lion-topped and inscribed pillars on his way to Lumbini—birthplace of the Buddha—in modern Nepal, where he encounters a sacred pool with an Ashokan pillar and stupa nearby. Outside Varanasi, he finds a column said to be 'as smooth as a mirror' and a huge stupa attributed to Ashoka. At Sarnath (the Deer Park monastery), where Buddha had given his transformative sermon to his first followers, he sees a huge temple, an Ashokan stupa, as well as yet another seventy-foot pillar, also described as mirror-like. He declares this to be the site where the Buddha attained enlightenment.

When he gets to Pataliputra, he discovers it to be virtually in ruins. He comes across a huge column alleged to mark the site of Ashoka's hellish prison; he also sees, south of the city, a big stupa collapsing into the ground.

After visiting the ruined Cock monastery, the site of Ashoka's final decline, he proceeds to Bodh Gaya and finds its temple and the Bodhi Tree in dire condition. He goes on to tell a story that is reminiscent of Paul's dramatic conversion in the Christian Book of Acts: in it, King Wuyou leads a crusade against Buddhism and Buddhist sites, including an attempt to destroy the Bodhi Tree. But the Bodhi Tree survives Brahmanical orders to have it burnt. When it flourishes once again, Wuyou rues his decision and orders the tree to be watered from then on. His queen, out of disbelief, tries to follow through on the Brahmans' demand, and has the tree cut down, but Wuyou prays earnestly and has the roots watered, and the tree again springs back to life. Xuanzang says that Wuyou then had a ten-feet-high stone fence erected around the tree, and that the fence still exists.

He writes that the Bodhi Tree was attacked again by the Bengal King Sasanka, a devotee of Shiva who hated Buddhism and did everything he could to destroy it. But a last descendant of King Wuyou, King Purnavarman, has the remaining roots richly irrigated, and the tree once again revives and grows tall. Purnavarman is said to have built a much higher fence, and Xuanzang says that he saw it, with the tree flourishing above the tall enclosure.

Obviously, all of these later accounts of Ashoka involve mythological elements and religious metaphors, but they reveal how he was known and admired over the centuries long after his reign. And they offer much to further confirm the archaeological evidence provided by the edicts, monuments, and stupas of Ashoka's singular achievement long ago.

Appendix

The Edicts

The best available translation of all the edicts of Ashoka that have been found to date are reproduced below by the courtesy of the translator, Ven. S. Dhammika.

'The Edicts of King Asoka',
an English rendering by
Ven. S. Dhammika
© 1994

Preface

This rendering of King Asoka's Edicts is based heavily on Amulyachandra Sen's English translation, which includes the original Magadhi and a Sanskrit and English translation of the text. However, many parts of the edicts are far from clear in meaning and the numerous translations of them differ widely. Therefore, I have also consulted the translations of C.D. Sircar and D.R. Bhandarkar and in parts favoured their interpretations. Any credit this small book deserves is due entirely to the labours and learning of these scholars.

The Fourteen Rock Edicts

1

Beloved-of-the-Gods, King Piyadasi, has caused this Dhamma edict to be written.[1] Here [in my domain] no living beings are to be slaughtered or offered in sacrifice. Nor should festivals be held, for Beloved-of-the-Gods, King Piyadasi, sees much to object to in such festivals, although there are some festivals that Beloved-of-the-Gods, King Piyadasi, does approve of.

Formerly, in the kitchen of Beloved-of-the-Gods, King Piyadasi, hundreds of thousands of animals were killed every day to make curry. But now with the writing of this Dhamma edict only three creatures, two peacocks and a deer are killed, and the deer not always. And in time, not even these three creatures will be killed.

2

Everywhere[2] within Beloved-of-the-Gods, King Piyadasi's domain, and among the people beyond the borders, the Cholas, the Pandyas, the Satiyaputras, the Keralaputras, as far as Tamraparni and where the Greek king Antiochos rules, and among the kings who are neighbours of Antiochos[3], everywhere has Beloved-of-the-Gods, King Piyadasi, made provision for two types of medical treatment: medical treatment for humans and medical treatment for animals. Wherever medical herbs suitable for humans or animals are not available, I have had them imported and grown. Along roads I have had wells dug and trees planted for the benefit of humans and animals.[4]

3

Beloved-of-the-Gods, King Piyadasi, speaks thus:[5] Twelve years after my coronation this has been ordered—Everywhere in my domain the Yuktas, the Rajjukas and the Pradesikas shall go on inspection tours every five years for the purpose of Dhamma instruction and also to conduct other business.[6]

Respect for mother and father is good, generosity to friends, acquaintances, relatives, Brahmans and ascetics is good, not killing living beings is good, moderation in spending and moderation in saving is good. The Council shall notify the Yuktas about the observance of these instructions in these very words.

4

In the past, for many hundreds of years, killing or harming living beings and improper behaviour towards relatives, and improper behaviour towards Brahmans and ascetics has increased.[7] But now due to Beloved-of-the-Gods, King Piyadasi's Dhamma practice, the sound of the drum has been replaced by the sound of the Dhamma.[8] The sighting of heavenly cars, auspicious elephants, bodies of fire and other divine sightings has not happened for many hundreds of years. But now because Beloved-of-the-Gods, King Piyadasi promotes restraint in the killing and harming of living beings, proper behaviour towards relatives, Brahmans and ascetics, and respect for mother, father and elders, such sightings have increased.[9]

These and many other kinds of Dhamma practice have been encouraged by Beloved-of-the-Gods, King Piyadasi, and he will continue to promote Dhamma practice. And the sons, grandsons and great-grandsons of Beloved-of-the-Gods, King

Piyadasi, too will continue to promote Dhamma practice until the end of time; living by Dhamma and virtue, they will instruct in Dhamma. Truly, this is the highest work, to instruct in Dhamma. But practicing the Dhamma cannot be done by one who is devoid of virtue and therefore its promotion and growth is commendable.

This edict has been written so that it may please my successors to devote themselves to promoting these things and not allow them to decline. Beloved-of-the-Gods, King Piyadasi, has had this written twelve years after his coronation.

5

Beloved-of-the-Gods, King Piyadasi, speaks thus:[10] To do good is difficult. One who does good first does something hard to do. I have done many good deeds, and, if my sons, grandsons and their descendants up to the end of the world act in like manner, they too will do much good. But whoever amongst them neglects this, they will do evil. Truly, it is easy to do evil.[11]

In the past there were no Dhamma Mahamatras but such officers were appointed by me thirteen years after my coronation. Now they work among all religions for the establishment of Dhamma, for the promotion of Dhamma, and for the welfare and happiness of all who are devoted to Dhamma. They work among the Greeks, the Kambojas, the Gandharas, the Rastrikas, the Pitinikas and other peoples on the western borders.[12] They work among soldiers, chiefs, Brahmans, householders, the poor, the aged and those devoted to Dhamma—for their welfare and happiness—so that they may be free from harassment. They [Dhamma Mahamatras] work for the proper treatment of prisoners, towards their unfettering, and if the Mahamatras think, 'This one has a family to support', 'That one has been bewitched', 'This one is old', then they work for the release of such prisoners. They work here, in outlying towns, in the women's quarters belonging to my brothers and sisters, and among my other relatives. They are occupied everywhere. These Dhamma Mahamatras are occupied in my domain among people devoted to Dhamma to determine who is devoted to Dhamma, who is established in Dhamma, and who is generous.

This Dhamma edict has been written on stone so that it might endure long and that my descendants might act in conformity with it.

6

Beloved-of-the-Gods, King Piyadasi, speaks thus:[13] In the past, state business was not transacted nor were reports delivered to the king at all hours. But now I have given this order, that at any time, whether I am eating, in the women's quarters, the bed chamber, the chariot, the palanquin, in the park or wherever, reporters are to be posted with instructions to report to me the affairs of the people so that I might attend to these affairs wherever I am. And whatever I orally order in connection with donations or proclamations, or when urgent business presses itself on the Mahamatras, if disagreement or debate arises in the Council, then it must be reported to me immediately. This is what I have ordered. I am never content with exerting myself or with dispatching business. Truly, I consider the welfare of all to be my duty, and the root of this is exertion and the prompt dispatch of business. There is no better work than promoting the welfare of all the people and whatever efforts I am making is to repay the debt I owe to all beings to assure their happiness in this life, and attain heaven in the next.

Therefore this Dhamma edict has been written to last long and that my sons, grandsons and great-grandsons might act in conformity with it for the welfare of the world. However, this is difficult to do without great exertion.

7

Beloved-of-the-Gods, King Piyadasi, desires that all religions should reside everywhere, for all of them desire self-control and purity of heart.[14] But people have various desires and various passions, and they may practice all of what they should or only a part of it. But one who receives great gifts yet is lacking in self-control, purity of heart, gratitude and firm devotion, such a person is mean.

8

In the past kings used to go out on pleasure tours during which there was hunting and other entertainment.[15] But ten years after Beloved-of-the-Gods had been coroneted, he went on a tour to Sambodhi and thus instituted Dhamma tours.[16] During these tours, the following things took place: visits and gifts to Brahmans and ascetics, visits and gifts of gold to the aged, visits to people in the countryside, instructing them in Dhamma, and discussing Dhamma with them as is suitable. It is this that delights Beloved-of-the-Gods, King Piyadasi, and is, as it were, another type of revenue.

9

Beloved-of-the-Gods, King Piyadasi, speaks thus:[17] In times of sickness, for the marriage of sons and daughters, at the birth of children, before embarking on a journey, on these and other occasions, people perform various ceremonies. Women in particular perform many vulgar and worthless ceremonies. These types of ceremonies can be performed by all means, but they bear little fruit. What does bear great fruit, however, is the ceremony of the Dhamma. This involves proper behaviour towards servants and employees, respect for teachers, restraint towards living beings, and generosity towards ascetics and Brahmans. These and other things constitute the ceremony of the Dhamma. Therefore a father, a son, a brother, a master, a friend, a companion and even a neighbour should say: 'This is good, this is the ceremony that should be performed until its purpose is fulfilled, this I shall do.'[18] Other ceremonies are of doubtful fruit, for they may achieve their purpose, or they may not, and even if they do, it is only in this world. But the ceremony of the Dhamma is timeless. Even if it does not achieve its purpose in this world, it produces great merit in the next, whereas if it does achieve its purpose in this world, one gets great merit both here and there through the ceremony of the Dhamma.

10

Beloved-of-the-Gods, King Piyadasi, does not consider glory and fame to be of great account unless they are achieved through having my subjects respect Dhamma and practice Dhamma, both now and in the future.[19] For this alone does Beloved-of-the-Gods, King Piyadasi, desire glory and fame. And whatever efforts Beloved-of-the-Gods, King Piyadasi, is making, all of that is only for the welfare of the people in the next world, and that they will have little evil. And being without merit is evil. This is difficult for either a humble person or a great person to do except with great effort, and by giving up other interests. In fact, it may be even more difficult for a great person to do.

11

Beloved-of-the-Gods, King Piyadasi, speaks thus:[20] There is no gift like the gift of the Dhamma[21] [no acquaintance like], acquaintance with Dhamma, [no distribution like] distribution of Dhamma, and [no kinship like] kinship through Dhamma. And it consists of this: proper behaviour towards servants and employees, respect for mother and father, generosity to friends, companions, relations, Brahmans and ascetics, and not killing living beings. Therefore a father, a son, a brother, a master, a friend, a companion or a neighbour should say: 'This is good, this should be done.' One benefits in this world and gains great merit in the next by giving the gift of the Dhamma.

12

Beloved-of-the-Gods, King Piyadasi, honours both ascetics and the householders of all religions, and he honours them with gifts and honours of various kinds.[22] But Beloved-of-the-Gods, King Piyadasi, does not value gifts and honours as much as he values this—that there should be growth in the essentials of all religions.[23] Growth in essentials can be done in different ways, but all of them have as their root restraint in speech, that is, not praising one's own religion or condemning the religion of others without good cause. And if there is cause for criticism, it should be done in a mild way. But it is better to honour other religions for this reason. By so doing, one's own religion benefits, and so do other religions, while doing otherwise harms one's own religion and the religions of others. Whoever praises his own religion, due to excessive devotion, and condemns others with the thought, 'Let me glorify my own religion', only harms his own religion. Therefore contact [between religions] is good.[24] One should listen to and respect the doctrines professed by others. Beloved-of-the-Gods, King Piyadasi, desires that all should be well-learned in the good doctrines of other religions.

Those who are content with their own religion should be told this: Beloved-of-the-Gods, King Piyadasi, does not value gifts and honours as much as he values that there should be growth in the essentials of all religions. And to this end many are working—Dhamma Mahamatras, Mahamatras in charge of the women's quarters, officers in charge of outlying areas, and other such officers. And the fruit of this is that one's own religion grows and the Dhamma is illuminated also.

13

Beloved-of-the-Gods, King Piyadasi, conquered the Kalingas eight years after his coronation.[25] One hundred and fifty thousand were deported, one hundred thousand were killed and many more died from other causes. After the Kalingas had been conquered, Beloved-of-the-Gods came to feel a strong inclination towards the Dhamma, a love for the Dhamma and for instruction in Dhamma. Now Beloved-of-the-Gods feels deep remorse for having conquered the Kalingas.

Indeed, Beloved-of-the-Gods is deeply pained by the killing, dying and deportation that take place when an unconquered country is conquered. But Beloved-of-the-Gods is pained even more by this—that Brahmans, ascetics, and householders of different religions who live in those countries, and who are respectful to superiors, to mother and father, to elders, and who behave properly and have strong loyalty towards friends, acquaintances, companions, relatives, servants and employees— that they are injured, killed or separated from their loved ones. Even those who are not affected [by all this] suffer when they see friends, acquaintances, companions and relatives affected. These misfortunes befall all [as a result of war], and this pains Beloved-of-the-Gods.

There is no country, except among the Greeks, where these two groups, Brahmans and ascetics, are not found, and there is no country where people are not devoted to one or another religion.[26] Therefore the killing, death or deportation of a hundredth, or even a thousandth part of those who died during the conquest of Kalinga now pains Beloved-of-the-Gods. Now Beloved-of-the-Gods thinks that even those who do wrong should be forgiven where forgiveness is possible.

Even the forest people, who live in Beloved-of-the-Gods' domain, are entreated and reasoned with to act properly. They are told that despite his remorse Beloved-of-the-Gods has the power to punish them if necessary, so that they should be ashamed of their wrong and not be killed. Truly, Beloved-of-the-Gods desires non-injury, restraint and impartiality to all beings, even where wrong has been done.

Now it is conquest by Dhamma that Beloved-of-the-Gods considers to be the best conquest.[27] And it [conquest by Dhamma] has been won here, on the borders, even six hundred yojanas away, where the Greek king Antiochos rules, beyond there where the four kings named Ptolemy, Antigonos, Magas and Alexander rule, likewise in the south among the Cholas, the Pandyas, and as far as Tamraparni.[28] Here in the king's domain among the Greeks, the Kambojas, the Nabhakas, the Nabhapamkits, the Bhojas, the Pitinikas, the Andhras and the Palidas, everywhere people are following Beloved-of-the-Gods' instructions in Dhamma. Even where Beloved-of-the-Gods' envoys have not been, these people too, having heard of the practice of Dhamma and the ordinances and instructions in Dhamma given by Beloved-of-the-Gods, are following it and will continue to do so. This conquest has been won everywhere, and it gives great joy—the joy which only conquest by Dhamma can give. But even this joy is of little consequence. Beloved-of-the-Gods considers the great fruit to be experienced in the next world to be more important.

I have had this Dhamma edict written so that my sons and great-grandsons may not consider making new conquests, or that if military conquests are made, that they be done with forbearance and light punishment, or better still, that they consider making conquest by Dhamma only, for that bears fruit in this world and the next. May all their intense devotion be given to this which has a result in this world and the next.

14

Beloved-of-the-Gods, King Piyadasi, has had these Dhamma edicts written in brief, in medium length, and in extended form.[29] Not all of them occur everywhere, for my domain is vast, but much has been written, and I will have still more written. And also there are some subjects here that have been spoken of again and again because of their sweetness, and so that the people may act in accordance with them. If some things written are incomplete, this is because of the locality, or in consideration of the object or due to the fault of the scribe.

The Kalinga Rock Edicts

1

Beloved-of-the-Gods says that the Mahamatras of Tosali who are judicial officers in the city are to be told this.[30] I wish to see that everything I consider to be proper is carried out in the right way. And I consider instructing you to be the best way of accomplishing this. I have placed you over many thousands of people that you may win the people's affection.

All men are my children. What I desire for my own children, and I desire their welfare and happiness both in this world and the next, that I desire for all men. You do not understand to what extent I desire this, and if some of you do understand, you do not understand the full extent of my desire.

You must attend to this matter. While being completely law-abiding, some people are imprisoned, treated harshly and even killed without cause so that many people suffer. Therefore your aim should be to act with impartiality. It is because of these things—envy, anger, cruelty, hate, indifference, laziness or tiredness—that such a thing does not happen. Therefore your aim should be: 'May these things not be in me'. And the root of this is non-anger and patience. Those who are bored with the administration of justice will not be promoted; [those who are not] will move upwards and be promoted. Whoever among you understands this should say to his colleagues: 'See that you do your duty properly. Such and such are Beloved-of-the-Gods' instructions.' Great fruit will result from doing your duty, while failing in it will result in gaining neither heaven nor the king's pleasure. Failure in duty on your part will not please me. But done properly, it will win you heaven and you will be discharging your debts to me.

This edict is to be listened to on Tisa day, between Tisa days, and on other suitable occasions, it should be listened to even by a single person. Acting thus, you will be doing your duty.

This edict has been written for the following purpose: that the judicial officers of the city may strive to do their duty and that the people under them might not suffer unjust imprisonment or harsh treatment. To achieve this, I will send out Mahamatras every five years who are not harsh or cruel, but who are merciful and who can ascertain if the judicial officers have understood my purpose and are acting according to my instructions. Similarly, from Ujjayini, the prince will send similar persons with the same purpose without allowing three years to elapse. Likewise from Takhasila also. When these Mahamatras go on tours of inspection each year, then without neglecting their normal duties, they will ascertain if judicial officers are acting according to the king's instructions.

2

Beloved-of-the-Gods speaks thus:[31] This royal order is to be addressed to the Mahamatras at Samapa. I wish to see that everything I consider to be proper is carried out in the right way. And I consider instructing you to be the best way of accomplishing this. All men are my children. What I desire for my own children, and I desire their welfare and happiness both in this world and the next, that I desire for all men.[32] The people of the unconquered territories beyond the borders might think: 'What is the king's intentions towards us?' My only intention is that they live without fear of me, that they may trust me and that I may give them happiness, not sorrow. Furthermore, they should understand that the king will forgive those who can be forgiven, and that he wishes to encourage them to practice Dhamma so that they may attain happiness in this world and the next. I am telling you this so that I may discharge the debts I owe, and that in instructing you, that you may know that my vow and my promise will not be broken. Therefore acting in this way, you should perform your duties and assure them [the people beyond the borders] that: 'The king is like a father. He feels towards us as he feels towards himself. We are to him like his own children.'

By instructing you and informing you of my vow and my promise I shall be applying myself in complete fullness to achieving this object[ive]. You are able indeed to inspire them with confidence and to secure their welfare and happiness in this world and the next, and by acting thus, you will attain heaven as well as discharge the debts you owe to me. And so that the Mahamatras can devote themselves at all times to inspiring the border areas with confidence and encouraging them to practice Dhamma, this edict has been written here.

This edict is to be listened to every four months on Tisa day, between Tisa days, and on other suitable occasions, it should be listened to even by a single person. Acting thus, you will be doing your duty.

Minor Rock Edicts
1

Beloved-of-the-Gods speaks thus:[33] It is now more than two and a half years since I became a lay-disciple, but until now I have not been very zealous.[34] But now that I have visited the Sangha for more than a year, I have become very zealous. Now the people in India who have not associated with the gods do so. This is the result of zeal and it is not just the great who can do this. Even the humble, if they are zealous, can attain heaven. And this proclamation has been made with this aim. Let both humble and great be zealous, let even those on the borders know and let zeal last long. Then this zeal will increase, it will greatly increase, it will increase up to one-and-a-half times. This message has been proclaimed two hundred and fifty-six times by the king while on tour.

2

Beloved-of-the-Gods speaks thus:[35] Father and mother should be respected and so should elders, kindness to living beings should be made strong and the truth should be spoken. In these ways, the Dhamma should be promoted. Likewise, a teacher should be honoured by his pupil and proper manners should be shown towards relations. This is an ancient rule that conduces to long life. Thus should one act. Written by the scribe Chapala.

3

Piyadasi, King of Magadha, saluting the Sangha and wishing them good health and happiness, speaks thus:[36] You know, reverend sirs, how great my faith in the Buddha, the Dhamma and Sangha is. Whatever, reverend sirs, has been spoken by Lord Buddha, all that is well-spoken.[37] I consider it proper, reverend sirs, to advise on how the good Dhamma should last long.

These Dhamma texts—*Extracts from the Discipline*, the *Noble Way of Life*, the *Fears to Come*, the *Poem on the Silent Sage*, the *Discourse on the Pure Life*, *Upatisa's Questions*, and the *Advice to Rahula*, which was spoken by the Buddha concerning false speech—these Dhamma texts, reverend sirs, I desire that all the monks and nuns may constantly listen to and remember.[38] Likewise the laymen and laywomen. I have had this written that you may know my intentions.

The Seven Pillar Edicts
1

Beloved-of-the-Gods speaks thus:[39] This Dhamma edict was written twenty-six years after my coronation. Happiness in this world and the next is difficult to obtain without much love for the Dhamma, much self-examination, much respect, much fear [of evil], and much enthusiasm. But through my instruction this regard for Dhamma and love of Dhamma has grown day by day, and will continue to grow. And my officers of high, low and middle rank are practicing and conforming to Dhamma, and are capable of inspiring others to do the same. Mahamatras in border areas are doing the same. And these are my instructions: to protect with Dhamma, to make happiness through Dhamma and to guard with Dhamma.

2

Beloved-of-the-Gods, King Piyadasi, speaks thus: Dhamma is good, but what constitutes Dhamma? [It includes] little evil, much good, kindness, generosity, truthfulness and purity. I have given the gift of sight in various ways.[40] To two-footed and four-footed beings, to birds and aquatic animals, I have given various things including the gift of life. And many other good deeds have been done by me.

This Dhamma edict has been written that people might follow it and it might endure for a long time. And the one who follows it properly will do something good.

3

Beloved-of-the-Gods, King Piyadasi, speaks thus: People see only their good deeds saying, 'I have done this good deed'. But they do not see their evil deeds saying, 'I have done this evil deed' or 'This is called evil'. But this [tendency] is difficult to see.[41] One should think like this: 'It is these things that lead to evil, to violence, to cruelty, anger, pride and jealousy. Let me not ruin myself with these things.' And further, one should think: 'This leads to happiness in this world and the next.'

4

Beloved-of-the-Gods speaks thus: This Dhamma edict was written twenty-six years after my coronation. My Rajjukas are working among the people, among many hundreds of thousands of people. The hearing of petitions and the administration of justice has been left to them so that they can do their duties confidently and fearlessly and so that they can work for the welfare, happiness and benefit of the people in the country. But they should remember what causes happiness and sorrow, and being themselves devoted to Dhamma, they should encourage the people in the country [to do the same], that they may attain happiness in this world and the next. These Rajjukas are eager to serve me. They also obey other officers who know my desires, who instruct the Rajjukas so that they can please me. Just as a person feels confident having entrusted his child to an expert nurse thinking: 'The nurse will keep my child well,' even so, the Rajjukas have been appointed by me for the welfare and happiness of the people in the country.

The hearing of petitions and the administration of justice have been left to the Rajjukas so that they can do their duties unperturbed, fearlessly and confidently. It is my desire that there should be uniformity in law and uniformity in sentencing. I even go this far, to grant a three-day stay for those in prison who have been tried and sentenced to death. During this time their relatives can make appeals to have the prisoners' lives spared. If there is none to appeal on their behalf, the prisoners can give gifts in order to make merit for the next world, or observe fasts. Indeed, it is my wish that in this way, even if a prisoner's time is limited, he can prepare for the next world, and that people's Dhamma practice, self-control and generosity may grow.

5

Beloved-of-the-Gods, King Piyadasi, speaks thus: Twenty-six years after my coronation various animals were declared to be protected—parrots, mainas, *aruna*, ruddy geese, wild ducks, *nandimukhas, gelatas,* bats, queen ants, terrapins, boneless fish, *vedareyaka, gangapuputaka, sankiya* fish, tortoises, porcupines, squirrels, deer, bulls, *okapinda,* wild ass, wild pigeons, domestic pigeons and all four-footed creatures that are neither useful nor edible.[42] Those nanny goats, ewes and sows, which are with young or giving milk to their young are protected, and so are young ones less than six months old. Cocks are not to be caponised, husks hiding living beings are not to be burnt and forests are not to be burnt either without reason or to kill creatures. One animal is not to be fed to another. On the three Caturmasis, the three days of Tisa and during the fourteenth and fifteenth of the Uposatha, fish are protected and not to be sold. During these days animals are not to be killed in the elephant reserves or the fish reserves either. On the eighth of every fortnight, on the fourteenth and fifteenth, on Tisa, Punarvasu, the three Caturmasis and other auspicious days, bulls are not to be castrated, billy goats, rams, boars and other animals that are usually castrated are not to be. On Tisa, Punarvasu, Caturmasis and the fortnight of Caturmasis, horses and bullocks are not be branded.

In the twenty-six years since my coronation prisoners have been given amnesty on twenty-five occasions.

6

Beloved-of-the-Gods speaks thus: Twelve years after my coronation I started to have Dhamma edicts written for the welfare and happiness of the people, and so that not transgressing them they might grow in the Dhamma. Thinking: 'How can the welfare and happiness of the people be secured?' I give attention to my relatives, to those dwelling near and those dwelling far, so I can lead them to happiness and then I act accordingly. I do the same for all groups. I have honoured all religions with various honours. But I consider it best to meet with people personally.

This Dhamma edict was written twenty-six years after my coronation.

7

Beloved-of-the-Gods speaks thus: In the past kings desired that the people might grow through the promotion of the Dhamma. But despite this, people did not grow through the promotion of the Dhamma. Beloved-of-the-Gods, King Piyadasi, said concerning this: 'It occurs to me that in the past kings desired that the people might grow through the promotion of the Dhamma. But despite this, people did not grow through the promotion of the Dhamma. Now how can the people be encouraged to follow it? How can the people be encouraged to grow through the promotion of the Dhamma? How can I elevate them by promoting the Dhamma?' Beloved-of-the-Gods, King Piyadasi, further said concerning this: 'It occurs to me that I shall have proclamations on Dhamma announced and instruction on Dhamma given. When people hear these, they will follow them, elevate themselves and grow considerably through the promotion of the Dhamma.' It is for this purpose that proclamations on Dhamma have been announced and various instructions on Dhamma have been given and that officers who work among many promote and explain them in detail. The Rajjukas who work among hundreds of thousands of people have likewise been ordered: 'In this way and that encourage those who are devoted to Dhamma.' Beloved-of-the-Gods speaks thus: 'Having this object in view, I have set up Dhamma pillars, appointed Dhamma Mahamatras, and announced Dhamma proclamations.'

Beloved-of-the-Gods, King Piyadasi, says: Along roads I have had banyan trees planted so that they can give shade to animals and men, and I have had mango groves planted. At intervals of eight *krosas,* I have had wells dug, rest-houses built, and in various places, I have had watering-places made for the use of animals and men. But these are but minor achievements.

Such things to make the people happy have been done by former kings. I have done these things for this purpose, that the people might practice the Dhamma.

Beloved-of-the-Gods, King Piyadasi, speaks thus: My Dhamma Mahamatras too are occupied with various good works among the ascetics and householders of all religions. I have ordered that they should be occupied with the affairs of the Sangha. I have also ordered that they should be occupied with the affairs of the Brahmans and the Ajivikas. I have ordered that they be occupied with the Niganthas.[43] In fact, I have ordered that different Mahamatras be occupied with the particular affairs of all different religions. And my Dhamma Mahamatras likewise are occupied with these and other religions.

Beloved-of-the-Gods, King Piyadasi, speaks thus: These and other principal officers are occupied with the distribution of gifts, mine as well as those of the queens. In my women's quarters, they organise various charitable activities here and in the provinces. I have also ordered my sons and the sons of other queens to distribute gifts so that noble deeds of Dhamma and the practice of Dhamma may be promoted. And noble deeds of Dhamma and the practice of Dhamma consist of having kindness, generosity, truthfulness, purity, gentleness and goodness increase among the people.

Beloved-of-the-Gods, King Piyadasi, speaks thus: Whatever good deeds have been done by me, those the people accept and those they follow. Therefore they have progressed and will continue to progress by being respectful to mother and father, respectful to elders, by courtesy to the aged and proper behaviour towards Brahmans and ascetics, towards the poor and distressed, and even towards servants and employees.

Beloved-of-the-Gods, King Piyadasi, speaks thus: This progress among the people through Dhamma has been done by two means, by Dhamma regulations and by persuasion. Of these, Dhamma regulation is of little effect, while persuasion has much more effect. The Dhamma regulations I have given are that various animals must be protected. And I have given many other Dhamma regulations also. But it is by persuasion that progress among the people through Dhamma has had a greater effect in respect of harmlessness to living beings and non-killing of living beings.

Concerning this, Beloved-of-the-Gods says: Wherever there are stone pillars or stone slabs, there this Dhamma edict is to be engraved so that it may long endure. It has been engraved so that it may endure as long as my sons and great-grandsons live and as long as the sun and the moon shine, and so that people may practice it as instructed. For by practicing it happiness will be attained in this world and the next.

This Dhamma edict has been written by me twenty-seven years after my coronation.

The Minor Pillar Edicts
1
Twenty years after his coronation, Beloved-of-the-Gods, King Piyadasi, visited this place and worshipped because here the Buddha, the sage of the Sakyans, was born.[44] He had a stone figure and a pillar set up and because the Lord was born here, the village of Lumbini was exempted from tax and required to pay only one eighth of the produce.

2
Beloved-of-the-Gods commands.[45] The Mahamatras at Kosambi [are to be told: Whoever splits the Sangha] which is now united, is not to be admitted into the Sangha. Whoever, whether monk or nun, splits the Sangha is to be made to

wear white clothes and to reside somewhere other than in a monastery.[46]

Notes

1. Girnar version issued in 257 B.C. These fourteen edicts, with minor differences, are found in five different places throughout India. In two other places, they are found minus numbers 11, 12 and 13.
2. Girnar version, issued in 257 B.C.
3. The Cholas and Pandyas were south Indian peoples living outside Asoka's empire. The Satiyaputras and Keralaputras lived on the southwest seaboard of India. Tamraparni is one of the ancient names for Sri Lanka. On Antiochos see Note 28.
4. By so doing, Asoka was following the advice given by the Buddha at Samyutta Nikaya, I:33.
5. Girnar version, issued in 257 B.C.
6. The exact duties of these royal officers are not known.
7. Girnar version, issued in 257 B.C.
8. This probably refers to the drum that was beaten to announce the punishment of lawbreakers. See Samyutta Nikaya, IV:244.
9. Like many people in the ancient world, Asoka believed that when a just king ruled, there would be many auspicious portents.
10. Kalsi version, issued in 256 B.C.
11. This seems to be a paraphrase of Dhammapada 163.
12. The Greeks (Yona) settled in large numbers in what is now Afghanistan and Pakistan after the conquests of Alexander the Great, although small communities lived there prior to this.

13. Girnar version, issued in 256 B.C.

14. Girnar version, issued in 256 B.C.

15. Girnar version, issued in 256 B.C.

16. Bodh Gaya, the site of the Buddha's enlightenment, was known in ancient times as either Sambodhi or Vajirasana.

17. Kalsi version, issued in 256 BC. Asoka obviously had the Mangala Sutta (Sutta Nipata 258-269) in mind when he issued this edict. The word here translated as ceremony is *mangala.*

18. Other versions substitute the following up to the end of the edict. It has also been said: 'Generosity is good'. But there is no gift or benefit like the gift of the Dhamma or benefit like the benefit of the Dhamma. There a friend, a well-wisher, a relative or a companion should encourage others thus on appropriate occasions: 'This should be done, this is good, by doing this, one can attain heaven.' And what greater achievement is there than this, to attain heaven?

19. Girnar version, issued in 256 BC.

20. Girnar version, issued in 256 BC

21. Similar to Dhammapada 354 BC

22. Girnar version, issued in 256 BC

23. Asoka probably believed that the essentials *(saravadi)* of all religions were their ethical principles.

24. *(Ta samavayo eva sadhu).* This sentence is usually translated as: 'Therefore concord is commendable.' *Samavayo,* however, comes from *sam + ava + i,* 'to come together'.

25. Kalsi version, issued in 256 BC. Kalinga corresponds roughly to the modern state of Odisha.

26. The Buddha pointed out that the four castes of Indian society likewise were not found among the Greeks; see Majjhima Nikaya, II:149.

27. Perhaps Asoka had in mind Dhammapada 103-104.

28. Antiochos II Theos of Syria (261-246 BC), Ptolemy II Philadelphos of Egypt (285-247 BC), Antigonos Gonatos of Macedonia (278-239 BC), Magas of Cyrene (300-258 BC) and Alexander of Epirus (272-258 BC).

29. Girnar version, issued in 256 BC.

30. Dhauli version, issued in 256 BC. These two edicts are found in two different places.

31. Dhauli version, issued in 256 BC.

32. This is reminiscent of the Buddha's words: 'Just as a mother would protect her only child even at the risk of her own life, even so, let one cultivate a boundless heart towards all beings.' Sutta Nipata 149.

33. Gavimath version, issued in 257 BC. This edict is found in twelve different places.

34. First Asoka was a lay-disciple *(upasaka)* and then he visited or literally 'went to the Sangha' *(yam me samghe upeti).* Some scholars think this means that Asoka became a monk. However it probably means that he started visiting Buddhist monks more often and listening to their instructions more carefully.

35. Brahmagiri version.

36. This edict was found inscribed on a small rock near the town of Bairat and is now housed at the Asiatic Society in Calcutta. Its date is not known.

37. This sentence is the converse of a similar one in the Tipitaka: '...that which is well-spoken is the words of the Lord.' Anguttara Nikaya, IV:164.

38. There is disagreement amongst scholars concerning which Pali suttas correspond to some of the text. Vinaya samukose: probably the Atthavasa Vagga, Anguttara Nikaya, 1:98-100. Aliya vasani: either the Ariyavasa Sutta, Anguttara Nikaya, V:29, or the Ariyavamsa Sutta, Anguttara Nikaya, II: 27-28.

Anagata bhayani: probably the Anagata Sutta, Anguttara Nikaya, III:100. Muni gatha: Muni Sutta, Sutta Nipata 207-221. Upatisa pasine: Sariputta Sutta, Sutta Nipata 955-975. Laghulavade: Rahulavada Sutta, Majjhima Nikaya, I:421.

39. The following seven edicts are from the Delhi Topra version, the first six being issued in 243 BC and the seventh in 242 BC. The first six edicts also appear on five other pillars.

40. *Cakhu dane.* The meaning is unclear. It may mean that Asoka has given 'the eye of wisdom', but taking into account the context, it more likely means he has stopped blinding as a form of punishment.

41. Similar to the ideas expressed by the Buddha in Dhammapada 50 and 252.

42. The identification of many of these animals is conjectural.

43. The Ajivikas were a sect of ascetics in ancient India established by Makkhali Gosala, a contemporary of the Buddha. The Niganthas are the Jains.

44. This inscription is found on a pillar in Lumbini where the Buddha was born. It was issued in 249 BC, probably at the time of Asoka's visit to the place.

45. Allahabad version, date of issue not known. The words in brackets are missing due to damage on the pillar, but they can be reconstructed from the three other versions of this edict.

46. The white clothes of the lay followers rather than the yellow robe of a monk or nun.

Bibliography

D.R. Bhandarkar, *Asoka*. Calcutta, 1955

R. Mookerji, *Asoka*. Delhi, 1962

A. Sen, *Asoka's Edicts*. Calcutta, 1956

A. Seneviratna (editor), *King Asoka and Buddhism*. Kandy, 1994
D.C. Sircar, *Inscriptions of Asoka*. Delhi, 1957.

'The Edicts of King Asoka' an English rendering by Ven. S. Dhammika. *Access to Insight (BCBS Edition)*, 30 November 2013, http://www.accesstoinsight.org/lib/authors/dhammika/wheel386.html

Access to Insight is owned and managed by the Barre Center for Buddhist Studies.

Endnotes

Chapter 1: Ashoka's Epiphany
The edict is taken from www.accesstoinsight.org/lib/authors/dhammika/ wheel386.html.

Chapter 2: Ashoka, an Introduction
1. H.G. Wells, *Outline of History*, Doubleday, 1971, p. 339.
2. B.M. Barua, *Asoka and His Inscriptions,* New Age Publishers, 1946, 1968, pp. 329–30.
3. Huston Smith and Philip Novak, *Buddhism: A Concise Introduction*, HarperCollins, 2004, pp. 117–118.
4. John S. Strong, *The Legend of King Asoka,* Motilal Banarsidass Publishers, 1983, 1989, 2002, p. 4.
5. N. Lahiri, *Ashoka in Ancient India*, Harvard University Press, 2015, pp. 18, 19.
6. Observed by Charles Allen in *Ashoka*, Overlook Press, 2012, p. 354.
7. These edicts have been paraphrased from V. A. Smith, *Asoka*, Clarendon Press, 1901. Chapter IV, pages 114–143.

Chapter 3: Discovering Ashoka
1. John S. Strong, *The Legend of King Asoka*, Motilal Banarsidass Publishers, 1989, p. 19.
2. M. McClish and P. Olivelle, *The Arthasastra*, Hackett Publishing, 2012, pp. xx, xxii, lxxi.
3. N. Lahiri, *Ashoka in Ancient India*, Harvard University Press, 2015, pp. 9, 60.

Chapter 4: Ashoka's Origins

1. D.P. Singhal, *India and World Civilization,* Michigan State University Press, 1969, p. 15, and *The Oxford History of India*, Oxford University Press, 1958, p. 103.
2. D.P. Singhal, *India and World Civilization,* Michigan State University Press, 1969, page 46.
3. R. Ghirshman, *Iran,* Pelican, 1954, and A.T. Olmstead, *History of the Persian Empire,* University of Chicago Press, 1948.
4. D.P. Singhal, *India and World Civilization,* Michigan State University Press, 1969, p. 27, where he quotes T. Gomperz, *Greek Thinkers.*
5. Plutarch, *Lives of the Noble Greeks*, Dell Classics,1959, p. 336.
6. R.K. Mookerji, *Chandragupta Maurya and His Times,* Motilal Banarsidass Publishers, 1943, p. 21.
7. J. Drèze and A. Sen, *An Uncertain Glory,* Princeton University Press, 2013, p. 76.
8. M. McClish and P. Olivelle, *The Arthasastra,* Hackett Publishing, 2012, p. xxx.
9. R. Thapar, *Asoka and the Decline of the Mauryas,* Oxford University Press, 1961, p. 129.
10. J. W. McCrindle, *Ancient India: As Described by Megasthenes and Arrian,* Chuckerverty, Chatterjee and Co. Ltd, 1926, p. 212. The text quotes Fa-Hien (Faxian), a Chinese traveller in the 5th century CE.
11. B.G. Gokhale, *Asoka Maurya,* Twayne Publishers, 1966, p. 32.
12. This version is based on a discussion with Professor P.S. Jaini at the University of California at Berkeley, USA.

Chapter 5: Ashoka

1. This section is a synthesis of three biographies about Ashoka by R. Thapar, V.A. Smith, and B.G. Gokhale, all cited earlier or later.
2. Charles Allen, *Ashoka,* Overlook Press, 2012, p. 344.
3. *The Economist,* November 16, 2013, p. 82, which contains a discussion of Dr I. Elia's article in the *Quarterly Review of Biology.*
4. John S. Strong, *The Legend of King Asoka,* Motilal Banarsidass Publishers, 1989, p. 206.
5. Other sources give different names, but the story remains similar (see R. Thapar, *Asoka and the Decline of the Mauryas,* Oxford University Press, 1961, p. 21).
6. Charles Allen, *Ashoka,* Overlook Press, 2012, pp. 375–376.
7. John S. Strong, *The Legend of King Asoka,* Motilal Banarsidass Publishers, 1989, pp. 40–41.
8. Andy Martin, 'The Phenomenology of Ugly', *New York Times*, August 10, 2010.

9. N. Lahiri, *Ashoka in Ancient India*, Harvard University Press, 2015, p. 68.

10. N. Lahiri, *Ashoka in Ancient India*, Harvard University Press, 2015, p. 93.

11. *Sanchi*, World Heritage Series, Archaeological Survey of India.

12. Another name for Ashoka after he became king, which means 'One who looks with kindness upon everything'.

13. Charles Allen, *Ashoka*, Overlook Press, 2012, p. 351.

14. The origin of the caste system in India and Nepal is shrouded in obscurity, but it seems to have originated some 2,000 years ago. Under this system, which is associated with Hinduism, people were categorised by their occupations. Although caste originally depended upon a person's work, it soon became hereditary. Each person was born into an unalterable social status. The four primary castes are: Brahman, the priests; Kshatriya, the warriors and nobility; Vaishya, the farmers, traders, and artisans; and Shudra, the tenant farmers and servants. Some people were born outside of (and below) the caste system. They were called 'untouchables'. See http://asianhistory.about.com/od/india/p/indiancastesystem.htmlxxx.

15. J. Drèze and A. Sen, *An Uncertain Glory*, Princeton University Press, 2013, p. 76.

16. Charles Allen, *Ashoka*, Overlook Press, 2012, p. 176.

17. Gautama is the family name of the person we know as Buddha, which means 'awakened'. There were Buddhas who lived before Gautama, but they are not well known.

18. Minor Rock Edict II is paraphrased from *Asoka* by Vincent Smith, Clarendon Press, 1901, p. 142.

19. S.J. Tambiah, *World Conqueror, World Renouncer*. Cambridge University Press, 1976, p. 58–63.

20. In 'Asoka's Inscriptions as Text and Ideology' by P. Olivelle in *Reimagining Asoka*, Oxford University Press, 2012, p. 173, 179.

21. N. Lahiri, *Ashoka in Ancient India*, Harvard University Press, 2015, pp. 138–139.

22. V.A. Smith, *Asoka*, Clarendon Press, 1901, p. 87.

23. Roy C. Craven, *A Concise History of Indian Art*, Praeger, 1976, p. 40.

24. B.G. Ghokale, 'Animal Symbolism in Early Buddhist Literature and Art', *East and West,* 24:1/2, 1974, pp. 111–120.

25. J.P. Vogel, *Buddhist Art in India*, quoted in B.G. Gokhale, op. cit., p. 138.

26. N. Lahiri, *Ashoka in Ancient India*, Harvard University Press, 2015, p. 284.

27. John Strong, 'Images of Asoka: Some Indian and Sri Lankan Legends and Their Development', in *King Asoka and Buddhism,* Buddhist Publication Society, 1994, p. 152.
28. N. Lahiri, *Ashoka in Ancient India*, Harvard University Press, 2015, p. 287.
29. The poem is from S.J. Tambiah, *The Buddhist Conception of Universal King and Its Manifestations in South and Southeast Asia*, University of Malaya, 1987, p. 61.
30. N. Lahiri, *Ashoka in Ancient India*, Harvard University Press, 2015, p. 287.

Chapter 6: The Decline and Fall of the Mauryan Empire

1. R. Thapar, *Asoka and the Decline of the Mauryas*, Oxford University Press, 1961, pp. 198–212.

Chapter 7: Ashoka's Legacy

1. John S. Strong, *The Legend of King Asoka*, Motilal Banarsidass Publishers, pp. 133.
2. These edicts and inscriptions are paraphrased from R. Thapar, *Asoka and the Decline of the Mauryas*, Oxford University Press, 1961, pp. 251–266.
3. B.G. Gokhale, *Asoka Maurya*, Twayne Publishers, 1966, p. 145.
4. Trevor Ling, *The Buddha,* Penguin Books, 1973, pp. 177–180.
5. S.J. Tambiah, *The Buddhist Conception of Universal King and its Manifestations in South and Southeast Asia*, University of Malaya, Kuala Lumpur, 1987, p. 24.
6. Trevor Ling, *The Buddha,* Penguin Books, 1973, pp. 224–229.
7. W.W. Tarn, *The Greeks in Bactria and India,* Cambridge University Press, 1951, pp. 262–264.
8. Frances Wood, *The Silk Road*, University of California Press, 2002, pp. 93–105.
9. This paragraph relies on M. Deeg, 'From the Iron Wheel to Bodhisattvahood: Asoka in Buddhist Culture and Memory', and in P. Olivelle, *Asoka: In History and Historical Memory*, pp. 122–132.
10. Thant Myint-U, *Where China Meets India,* Faber and Faber, 2012, pp. 167–168.
11. N. Lahiri, *Ashoka in Ancient India*, Harvard University Press, 2015, pp. 298–9.
12. The legends of Shwedagon Paya and Pha That Luang are from Lonely Planet guidebooks for those countries and H.P. Ray in 'Archaeology and Asoka' in *Reimagining Asoka*, Editors P. Olivelle, J. Leoshko, and H.P. Ray, Oxford University Press 2012, p. 75.

13. M. Deeg, 'Ashoka: Model Ruler Without a Name' in *Reimagining Ashoka*, Editors P. Olivelle, J. Leoshko, and H.P. Ray, Oxford University Press 2012, p. 372.

14. M. Sarkisyanz, 'On the Place of U Nu's Buddhist Socialism in Burma's History of Ideas', *Studies on Asia*, Series 1, Volume 2, 1961, pp. 59–60.

15. C.F. Keyes, L. Kendall, and H. Hardacre, *Asian Visions of Authority*, University of Hawaii Press, 1994, p. 53.

16. Ian Harris, *The Illustrated Encyclopedia of Buddhism*, Lorenz, 2009, p. 114.

17. William Hart, with S.N. Goenka, *The Art of Living*, Harper Collins, 1987, p. 8.

18. N. Lahiri, *Ashoka in Ancient India*, Harvard University Press, 2015, Lahiri, pp. 13–14.

19. R. Guha, *India After Gandhi*, Harper Collins Publishers, 2007, p. 622.

20. R. Guha, *India After Gandhi*, Harper Collins Publishers, 2007, p. 644.

21. M. McClish and P. Olivelle, *The Arthasastra*, Hackett Publishing, 2012, p. liii.

22. http://info.worldbank.org/governanCE/wgi/#faq-2.

23. P. French, *India: A Portrait*, Penguin, 2011, pp. 119–120.

Select Bibliography

www.accesstoinsight.org/lib/authors/dhammika/wheel386.html.

http://asianhistory.about.com/od/india/p/indiancastesystem.html.

Allen, C. *Ashoka: In Search for India's Lost Emperor.* Overlook Press, 2012.

Basham, A.L. *The Wonder That Was India*, Third Edition. Taplinger Publishing Co. Inc., 1968.

Bhandarkar, D.R. *Asoka: BC 273–BC 232.* University of Calcutta, 1925.

Drèze, J. and Sen, A. *An Uncertain Glory.* Princeton University Press, 2013.

Erikson, E. H. *Life History and the Historical Moment.* W.W. Norton & Co., 1975.

Erikson, E.H. *Identity and the Life Cycle.* W. W. Norton & Co., 1980.

Geiger, W. & Bode, M.H., translators. *Mahavamsa: The Great Chronicle of Ceylon.* Oxford University Press, 1912.

Ghirshman, R. *Iran.* Pelican, 1954.

Gokhale, B.G. *Asoka Maurya.* Twayne Publishers, 1966.

Guha, R. *India After Gandhi.* Harper Collins Publishers, 2007.

Keay, J. *A History of India.* Harper Collins Publishers, 2000.

Keyes, C.F., et al. *Asian Visions of Authority: Religion and the Modern States of East and Southeast Asia.* University of Hawaii Press, 1994.

Lahiri, N. *Ashoka in Ancient India.* Harvard University Press, 2015.

McCrindle, J.W. *Ancient India: As Described by Megasthenes and Arrian.* Chuckerverty, Chatterjee and Co. Ltd, 1926.

McClish, M. and Olivelle, P. editors, *The Arthasastra*, Hackett Publishing Company, 2012.

Modak, E.S. *Beloved of the Gods.* Rupa Publications, Pvt. Ltd., 2010.

Mookerji, R.K. *Chandragupta Maurya and His Times.* Motilal Banarsidass Publishers, 1943.

Olivelle, P., et al, editors, *Reimagining Asoka.* Oxford University Press, 2012.

Olmstead, A.T. *History of the Persian Empire.* University of Chicago Press, 1948.

Plutarch. *Lives of the Noble Greeks.* Dell Classics, 1959.

Rapson, E.J., Editor. *The Cambridge History of India, Volume I, Ancient India.* S. Chand & Co, 1968.

Ray, H. P. *The Return of the Buddha.* Routledge, 2014.

Rich, B. *To Uphold the World.* Viking, 2008.

Robinson, R, Johnson, W, Thanissaro, Bhikku. *Buddhist Religions: A Historical Introduction.* Fifth Edition. Thompson Wadsworth, 2005.

Sarkisyanz, M. *On the Place of U Nu's Buddhist Socialism in Burma's History of Ideas,* in Studies on Asia, Series 1, Volume 2, 1961.

Seneviratna, A., Editor. *King Asoka and Buddhism.* Buddhist Publication Society, 1994.

Singhal, D.P. *India and World Civilization.* Michigan State University Press, 1969.

Sircar, D.C. *Inscriptions of Asoka.* Ganges Printing Company, 1975.

Smith, V.A. *Asoka.* Clarendon Press, 1901.

Spear, P., Editor. *The Oxford History of India.* Oxford University Press, Third Edition, 1958.

Strong, J. *The Legend of King Asoka.* Motilal Banarsidass Publishers, 1989.

Tambiah, S. *World Conqueror, World Renouncer.* Cambridge University Press, 1976.

Thapar, R. *Asoka and the Decline of the Mauryas.* Oxford University Press, Second Edition, 1997.

The Oxford History of India, Third Edition, Oxford University Press, 1958.

Jayal, N.G., et al, Editors. *The Oxford Companion to Politics in India.* Oxford University Press, 2010.

Wells, H.G. *Outline of History.* Doubleday, 1971.

Index

Acknowledgements

This book has been on my mind for a very long time. Many friends encouraged me to continue my on-and-off research while earning a living. Even when I became free of that responsibility, progress was slow. Surit Mitra encouraged me to keep going and introduced me to Bloomsbury Publishing India, who gave me a contract that set a deadline for completion. Surit provided invaluable support by liaising with Bloomsbury during the publishing process. John Loudon's experienced editorial guidance and research helped me with the last mile to complete the book and Jordan Bass polished it at the end. Rishiraj Bhowmick and Himanshu Singh provided some research assistance from India. Venerable Dhammika kindly allowed me to include his translation of Ashoka's edicts. Robert Holmes enhanced my photographs for publication and Amitabha Bhattacharya helped by taking a needed photograph.